THE
WESTERN MOVIE
QUIZ BOOK

BY GRAEME ROSS

Published in the USA by:

BEARMANOR MEDIA
P.O. BOX 71426
ALBANY, GEORGIA 31708
www.BearManorMedia.com

IMAGES COPYRIGHT:
Many of the images contained in *The Western Movie Quiz Book* come from the author's own
collection. I am also grateful to www.doctormacro.com for the use of other images in the book.
Every effort has been made to identify correctly the rights holders and/or production companies
with respect to the images. If despite these efforts any attribution is incorrect and are brought
to our attention, they will be corrected on a subsequent reprint.

COVER CREDITS
FRONT—El Dorado Paramount Pictures/Laurel Productions
REAR—Vera Cruz United Artists

ILLUSTRATIONS
401 Universal 402 Republic Pictures 403 United Artists
404 Samuel Goldwyn Productions/United Artists 405 Twentieth Century Fox
406 Twentieth Century Fox 407 Paramount Pictures 408 Warner Brothers 409 Universal
410 Pathe America 611 High Noon United Artists 612 Twentieth Century Fox
618 United Artists 851 United Artists 852 Mulberry Square Productions
854 RKO Pictures 859 Paramount Pictures

ISBN-10: 1-59393-561-7 (alk. paper)
ISBN-13: 978-1-59393-561-0 (alk. paper)

DESIGN AND LAYOUT: VALERIE THOMPSON

TABLE OF CONTENTS

DEDICATION
This book is dedicated to all the great professionals both in front of and behind the camera who have contributed to the greatest movie genre of them all.

FOREWORD

BY **PHILIP FRENCH**, FILM CRITIC OF THE
OBSERVER AND AUTHOR OF *WESTERNS: ASPECTS OF A
MOVIE GENRE AND WESTERNS REVISITED*

This book features two of my great loves: westerns and quizzes. I saw my first films in 1937, and the cowboy movies made the greatest impression—the landscape, the action, the sense of freedom that belonged to men riding west, tall in the saddle. But I cannot put a title to any western before 1939 when I was six. From that year I have vivid memories of John Wayne shooting it out with the Plummer boys in the night streets of Lordsburg in John Ford's *Stagecoach* and of Tyrone Power being shot in the back by John Carradine as he puts up a picture on the wall in *Jesse James.* Carradine was also in *Stagecoach* as Hatfield, the elegant Southern gambler, so there's quiz material right there.

The radio was full of quiz shows as I grew up during world war two, and the one that had a special impact on me was *Transatlantic Quiz.* It ran on the BBC Home Service for over 100 editions from April 1944 to 1947 when it gave way to *Round Britain Quiz.* The hosts in New York and London were, respectively, Alistair Cooke—then on the point of attaining his legendary international renown—and Lionel Hale, with whom I later worked at the BBC. Various people made guest appearances in *Transatlantic Quiz,* among them, on the British side, Captain David Niven, who'd quit Hollywood in 1939 to rejoin the army; Peter Ustinov, also in the army but as a rather privileged private soldier; and the man Graham Greene called "unquestionably our best thriller writer," Lieutenant Colonel Eric Ambler. All three of them involved in one of the greatest British films of the war: *The Way Ahead.*

The star of *Transatlantic Quiz*, however, was unquestionably Sir Denis Brogan (then DW Brogan), the Cambridge don and renowned authority on French and American history who was on the British team for virtually every edition. Brogan's knowledge of America, its culture both high and popular, was phenomenal, encyclopaedic. He could unravel the most complicated question and then embroider his answer with further odd and recondite facts. He could turn his sharp, unpatronising mind to any aspect of US life past and present, and I later discovered that during the war he'd written a hard-boiled American thriller while confined for a couple of weeks in a hospital bed. He published it pseudonymously under the splendidly tough title *Stop on the Green Light*. I admired Brogan, learnt things every week from listening attentively to his answers, and I wanted to emulate his knowledge. Of course I never came anywhere near to matching his formidable erudition. But then, who did? I also never came close to matching his capacity for liquor, though I envied that too. So my youthful love of Hollywood movies and American comics became, through *Transatlantic Quiz*, a much larger fascination with American history and Americana, and also a critical one. It is this kind of knowledge I brought to bear on the scrutiny of movies and, in particular, the understanding and interpretation of westerns. I came to agree with a pronouncement of another great twentieth-century historian, Arthur M Schlesinger Jr. He once observed, when moonlighting as a film critic during his time as a special White House advisor during Jack Kennedy's presidency: "The western remains, I suppose, America's distinctive contribution to the film." Subsequently, in my professional life, quizzes became a part of my job: first at the BBC when I produced a transatlantic quiz programme between British and American students, and later on as I began setting quizzes on the past year's films in the Christmas editions of *The Observer*. As my children grew up, such playful interrogations became crucial to their mealtime discourse, a key element in their learning process. As a happy consequence, my three sons got together in 1992 to produce *The French Brothers Wild and Crazy Film Quiz Book* (Faber).

So reading Graeme Ross's attractive *The Western Movie Quiz Book* brought me great pleasure, not merely through immersing me in my favourite movie genre but by taking me down the dusty trail of memory lane and reminding me of what shaped me as a critic. I hope that wrestling with the questions will prod you into remembering the endless delights a century of westerns has brought you. I equally hope that consulting the answers will lead to new enjoyment through the discovery of westerns you haven't come across before. "Happy trails!" as they used to sing at the end of *The Roy Rogers Show*.

INTRODUCTION

Movie fads and trends come and go, but there will always be a place in the hearts of true film buffs for the western movie. The western is the most celebrated movie genre of all—almost as old as cinema itself. It is responsible for some of the most enduring images and iconic screen figures in the history of motion pictures. The west really did exist, and much of it still exists, but if the silver screen's portrayal of the events and characters of the real west are rooted more in myth than reality, then that's Hollywood. Most of the myths are just that—more fantasy than history. But we don't care. We are comfortable with the "man's gotta do what a man's gotta do" coda of Hollywood's west. A line from John Ford's *The Man Who Shot Liberty Valance* sums it up: "This is the west, sir. When the legend becomes fact, print the legend." The western is America's own wonderful gift to cinema, but what began as a uniquely American art form now has universal appeal, and film makers across the world have embraced and celebrated the genre. The western in some way has touched many of us—be it speech, dress, or the visual beauty of the landscapes. The vast terrains and landscapes of the American West demanded to be filmed. Step forward artists such as John Ford and Anthony Mann who created unforgettable visual tableaux, and icons like Wayne, Cooper, Stewart, and Eastwood, all of whom bestrode the screen as impressively as any of the natural wonders. And it's thanks to Hollywood that the western has left such an imprint on the world. The west and motion pictures have been as one, creating a world with its own language, dress, and moral code. So, what makes for a successful western and why do we love them so much? Well, we don't watch them for a history lesson. Even revisionist westerns, which show the west as the violent, squalid, unglamorous place it really was, don't aim for historical accuracy. The stock characters and ingredients of the western are long established, and the oft quoted "Gruber's Law" that there are only seven basic plots in the western still holds true to an extent. However, if ever there was an example of something that can be simple and one dimensional on the surface but complex underneath then it is the western, resulting in multiple sub plots and sub genres. Perhaps our love affair with horse operas goes back to childhood when the western movie and its television offspring were a ubiquitous, comforting presence in our homes. Perhaps it is because it transported us to a world that may never have existed, but feels like it should have. In the end, the appeal of the western may just be down to the happiest of accidents. The vital ingredients—myth, storyline, scenery, music, and sheer artistry—all fall into place to move us in ways we cannot fully articulate, but we just know that it feels and looks right. And the best westerns have a feel-good quality that is comforting when times are hard. And, in today's uncertain world, there is a revival of interest in the western. Westerns are still being made, and the DVD revolution and plethora of books on the genre ensures that they will not be forgotten. I hope that *The Western Movie Quiz Book* will, in some small way, help to keep the western legacy alive.

THE WESTERN:
A BRIEF HISTORY

The first western films were extensions of the "dime" novels of the 1880s, which romanticized real-life figures such as Wyatt Earp, "Wild" Bill Hickok, and Buffalo Bill Cody. However, they were handicapped by their eastern locations, and it was only the move west to California, and the development of Hollywood, which proved crucial in the rise of the western. The western quickly became popular—how could it fail? It had the locations, simple plotlines, action, and immediacy, given that many of the characters and events portrayed were still fresh in the minds of the audience. Hollywood grew during the silent years, and many memorable silent movies were westerns: *The Squaw Man*, directed by Cecil B. DeMille; *The Vanishing American*; and *The Iron Horse*, John Ford's first declaration of intent.

The western adapted easily enough to sound, with a young Gary Cooper establishing himself as a western star in *The Virginian*, and *Cimarron* winning best picture Oscar in 1931. The depression years witnessed a downturn in the big-budget western's fortunes however, although the "B" western became phenomenally popular during this time. They were of little artistic worth but allowed the likes of John Wayne to learn their trade in these "Poverty Row" fillers. Wayne finally came good in 1939 in John Ford's western classic *Stagecoach*. Credited with reviving the genre, *Stagecoach* was influential on many levels: the ensemble cast; innovative interior sets; exciting stunts; rescue by the cavalry; and the use of Monument Valley— possibly the single most recognizable location in western films. With world war two, the western lost much of its innocence, and film makers now adopted a more realistic, adult approach. *Duel in the Sun* and *The Outlaw* introduced sex into the western, William Wellman's *The Ox-bow Incident* was a message film about the evils of lynching, and *Pursued* was a film noir western. These westerns typified Hollywood's shift towards a more cynical view of the world, far removed from the simple values of the early westerns. Ford, as ever, stuck to the myth with his highly romanticised view of Wyatt Earp in the picaresque *My Darling Clementine.*

The western now entered its golden period, and many of the greatest westerns were made between 1946 and 1960. *Red River, Shane, High Noon, The Searchers, The Gunfighter, The Magnificent Seven* . . . the list goes on and on. Ironically, at this high water mark the western faced its greatest challenge as television introduced a plethora of horse operas that threatened to swamp the cinematic equivalent. Such was the impact and influence of the television westerns that when Gene Roddenberry was trying to raise interest in his Star Trek venture, he pitched it as "Wagon Train to the Stars." One film helped reverse the trend; *The Magnificent Seven*, released in 1960, was a huge international success, and it pointed the way towards Sergio Leone's spaghetti westerns with Clint Eastwood. Sergio Leone's Dollars trilogy reinvented the genre and gave rise to a more explicit violence. Sam Peckinpah picked up the gauntlet and showed the death of the old west in shocking detail in his blood-splattered masterpiece *The Wild Bunch.* The same year (1969) showed that Hollywood was still capable of combining rose-tinted nostalgia with the new realism in *Butch Cassidy and the Sundance Kid.*

The 1970s saw a massive reduction in the number of westerns produced, but great westerns were still being made, and any decade that produced *The Outlaw Josey Wales, Ulzana's Raid,* and *The Shootist* deserves respect. The death of John Wayne in 1979 seemed to presage the death of the western, and the 1980s certainly witnessed a terminal decline in the western's fortunes. Ironically, it was the landmark 1989 television miniseries *Lonesome Dove* that proved there was still an audience for the western, prompting renewed interest from film studios. Against the odds, two heroes—Costner and Eastwood—rode to the rescue, and the western made a comeback of sorts in the 1990s. Both *Dances with Wolves* and *Unforgiven* won best picture Oscars, proving there was a future for the western in the right hands. This renewed interest has continued, and in the twenty-first century the western lives on in fairly robust health. Most recently, we have seen new versions of *3.10 to Yuma*, *True Grit*, and *The Lone Ranger*, and as I write there is a mooted remake of *Westworld* for both film and television, and a possible adaption of Cormac McCarthy's *Blood Meridian* is in the pipeline. Quentin Tarantino entered the western fray in 2012 with the fabulously successful *Django Unchained*, and 2014 sees the return of Tommy Lee Jones to the western as both star and director of *The Homesman* from the impeccable source novel by Glendon Swarthout. Television has given us the notorious *Deadwood*, which took western revisionism to a whole new level, and the more traditional *Hell on Wheels*. The western's influence can be found widely in popular culture. What was *Star Wars* if it wasn't a western in space? And was Han Solo not the archetypal gunslinger? Bringing that analogy more up to date, and in the best Star Trek tradition, the cult sci-fi series *Firefly* and its spin-off movie *Serenity* wore their western influences very much on their sleeves. The western lives on!

CHAPTERS

1. OPENING LINES

Can you identify the western movie from these opening lines?

1.   "Somebody's coming pa."

2.   "My name is Joe Harmony. This is my stampin' ground."

3.   "I was Sheriff of this county when I was twenty-five years old. Hard to believe."

4.   "He was growing into middle age and was living then in a bungalow on Woodland Avenue."

5.   "Just where is it I can find bear, beaver, and other critters worth cash money when skinned?"

6.   "They come closer every day Pa."

7.   "Do not drink wine nor strong drink, thou nor thy sons with thee least ye shall die..."

8.   "Joe, you're under arrest."

9.   "Sorry old timer, but you're only part poison and I'm hungry for meat."

10.   "I am beyond doubt, the last of the old timers."

2. JESSE JAMES

Can you name the actors who have played the famous outlaw Jesse James in these films?

11. *Jesse James* (1939)

12. *The True Story of Jesse James* (1957)

13. *The Great Northfield Minnesota Raid* (1972)

14. *Best of the Badmen* (1951)

15. *The Assassination of Jesse James by the Coward Robert Ford* (2007)

16. *Alias Jesse James* (1959)

17. *American Outlaws* (2001)

18. *I Shot Jesse James* (1949)

19. *Jesse James Meets Frankenstein's Daughter* (1966)

20. *Frank and Jesse* (1995)

3. TITLE ROLES

Who played the title character in these westerns?

21. *Jeremiah Johnson* (1972)

22. *Major Dundee* (1964)

23. *Jubal* (1956)

24. *Belle Star* (1941)

25. *Alvarez Kelly* (1966)

26. *Cattle Queen of Montana* (1954)

27. *Yellowstone Kelly* (1959)

28. *The Cimarron Kid* (1952)

29. *Young Billy Young* (1969)

30. *Johnny Guitar* (1954)

4. NAME THE DIRECTOR

Can you name the directors of these classic western Movies?

31. *The Oxbow Incident* (1943)

32. *Shane* (1953)

33. *High Noon* (1952)

34. *Broken Arrow* (1950)

35. *The Gunfighter* (1950)

36. *The Big Country* (1958)

37. *Duel at Diablo* (1966)

38. *Hombre* (1967)

39. *Ulzana's Raid* (1972)

40. *The Long Riders* (1980)

5. LEADING LADIES

Can you recall the actresses who played the leading lady in these westerns?

41.   *The Wind* (1928)

42.   *They Died with Their Boots On* (1941)

43.   *Pursued* (1947)

44.   *The Bravados* (1958)

45.   *Winchester '73* (1950)

46.   *The Indian Fighter* (1955)

47.   *Rio Bravo* (1959)

48.   *Will Penny* (1968)

49.   *Butch Cassidy and the Sundance Kid* (1969)

50.   *Open Range* (2003)

6. WESTERN TRIVIA 1

51.   Can you name the four actors who played the *Sons of Katie Elder* in 1965?

52.   What was *True Grit's* Rooster Coburn's real Christian name?

53.   From which famous book was the story of Nevada Smith taken for the movie starring Steve McQueen in 1966?

54.   In *The Westerner* (1940), Judge Roy Bean was in love with which actress?

55.   Which actress donned a blonde wig for her role in *Heller in Pink Tights* (1960)?

56.   Name the western that was Elvis Presley's first film.

57.   What was the occupation of *The Lusty Men* (1952)?

58.   Which singer/songwriter wrote and recorded the song "Frank and Jesse James?"

59.   Can you name the movie in which Ronald Reagan played George Armstrong Custer?

60.   Can you name the actor, later to become famous for his spoof comedies, who played the villainous rancher in *The Sheepman* in 1958?

7. WESTERN QUOTES

Which actors spoke these memorable lines, and in which movies?

61.   "How come I've got to run into a squirt like you nearly every place I go these days?"

62.   "There's some things a man just can't ride around."

63.   "Brave men run in my family!"

64.   "If they move, kill 'em!"

65.   "When you call me that stranger, smile!"

66.   '"Damn that Texan, when you need him he's dead!"

67.   "All I want is to enter my house justified."

68.   "We deal in lead, friend."

69.   "You would do it for Randolph Scott!"

70.   "You crazy? The fall will probably kill you!"

8. WYATT EARP

Can you recall the actors who played the famous lawman Wyatt Earp in these movies?

71.   *Frontier Marshall* (1939)

72.   *My Darling Clementine* (1946)

73.   *Winchester '73* (1950)

74.   *Gun Belt* (1953)

75.   *Law and Order* (1955)

76.   *Gunfight at the OK Corral* (1957)

77.   *Alias Jesse James* (1959)

78.   *The Hour of the Gun* (1967)

79.   *Doc* (1971)

80.   *Watt Earp* (1994)

9. REAL NAMES

Can you match the western stars with their real names?

81.	Ray Milland	Ira Grossel
82.	Robert Taylor	Charles Carter
83.	Kirk Douglas	Louis Burton Lindley Junior
84.	Jack Palance	Leonard Slye
85.	Charlton Heston	Jerome Silberman
86.	Jeff Chandler	Volodymyr Palahniuk
87.	Slim Pickens	Roy Scherer Junior
88.	Gene Wilder	Spangler Arlington Brugh
89.	Roy Rogers	Issur Danielovitch
90.	Rock Hudson	Reginald Truscott Jones

10. WESTERN TRIVIA 2

91.   Which actor played Frank James in *The True Story of Jesse James* (1957)?

92.   Can you name the Errol Flynn western that is credited with having the greatest ever barroom brawl?

93.   Can you name the 1972 western that shares the name of a 1970s British rock band?

94.   Which actor played cowboy star Tom Mix in *Sunset* (1988)?

95.   What was the real name of the title character of *Nevada Smith* (1966)?

96.   Who was famously cast as a robotic gunfighter in the sci-fi movie *Westworld* in 1972?

97.   Can you name the famous western horse that made his movie debut as the mount of Maid Marian in *The Adventures of Robin Hood* in 1938?

98.   Who played Captain Jack, the Modoc Indian leader, in 1954's *Drumbeat*?

99.   What was the occupation of Jim McKay (Gregory Peck) in *The Big Country* (1958)?

100.   Who changed his name from Harold J. Smith and achieved fame on the small screen as a masked avenger's sidekick?

11. WESTERN OSCARS

Can you name the actors who won Oscars for their performances in these westerns?

101.   *In Old Arizona* (1929)

102.   *High Noon* (1952)

103.   *True Grit* (1969)

104.   *Unforgiven* (1992)

105.   *Viva Zapata!* (1952)

106.   *Stagecoach* (1939)

107.   *The Westerner* (1940)

108.   *City Slickers* (1991)

109.   *The Big Country* (1958)

110.   *Cat Ballou* (1965)

12. SOUNDTRACKS

Can you name the composers of the soundtracks of these westerns?

111. *The Big Country* (1958)

112. *The Magnificent Seven* (1960)

113. *Once Upon a Time in the West* (1968)

114. *Dances with Wolves* (1990)

115. *The Long Riders* (1980)

116. *Pat Garrett and Billy the Kid* (1973)

117. *Red River* (1948)

118. *The Missouri Breaks* (1976)

119. *Butch Cassidy and the Sundance Kid* (1969)

120. *Tombstone* (1993)

13. BAD GUYS

Who played these bad guys, and for an extra point can you name the movies they appeared in?

121.   Cicero Grimes

122.   Frank Miller

123.   Dad Longworth

124.   Jack Wilson

125.   Dutch Henry Brown

126.   Scar

127.   Deputy Sheriff Gutierrez

128.   Little Bill Daggett

129.   Clint Hollister

130.   Tully Crow

14. GOOD GUYS

Can you name the actors who played "the guy in the white hat" in these movies?

131.   Jesse McCanles in *Duel in the Sun* (1946)

132.   Chris Adams in *The Magnificent Seven* (1960)

133.   Ben Warren in *Gun Fury* (1953)

134.   Joe Starrett in *Shane* (1953)

135.   Jess Remsberg in *Duel at Diablo* (1966)

136.   Sandy McKenzie in *The Last Hunt* (1956)

137.   Captain Del Stewart in *The Man from Colorado* (1948)

138.   Hawkeye in *The Last of the Mohicans* (1932)

139.   Seven Ways from Sundown Jones in *Seven Ways from Sundown* (1960)

140.   Gil Carter in *The Oxbow Incident* (1943)

15. TELEVISION WESTERNS 1

Can you remember the television horse operas that these characters appeared in?

141.   Ben Cartwright

142.   Harry Briscoe

143.   Al Swearengen

144.   Jim Hardie

145.   Trampas

146.   Jake Spoon

147.   Paladin

148.   John Cannon

149.   Kitty Russell

150.   Major Seth Adams

16. THE FILM OF THE BOOK

Can you name the authors of the original books upon which these movies were based?

151.   *The Shootist* (1976)

152.   *True Grit* (1969 and 2010)

153.   *The Missing* (2003)

154.   *The Searchers* (1956)

155.   *The Oxbow Incident* (1943)

156.   *Shane* (1953)

157.   *Hombre* (1967)

158.   *The Virginian* (1929 and 1946)

159.   *Little Big Man* (1970)

160.   *Hondo* (1953)

17. WESTERN WOMEN

Can you recall the actresses who played these feisty females?

161. Vance Jeffords in *The Furies* (1950)

162. Hannie Caulder in *Hannie Caulder* (1971)

163. Joey MacDonald in *El Dorado* (1966)

164. Mattie Ross in *True Grit* (1969)

165. Ellen (The Lady) in *The Quick and the Dead* (1995)

166. Lola Manners in *Winchester '73* (1950)

167. Tess Millay in *Red River* (1948)

168. Josie Minick in *The Ballad of Josie* (1968)

169. Emma Small in *Johnny Guitar* (1954)

170. Ma Callum in *Pursued* (1947)

18. NATIVE AMERICANS 1

Can you name the Native American tribes featured in these westerns?

171.   *The Unforgiven* (1960)

172.   *The Searchers* (1956)

173.   *Broken Arrow* (1950)

174.   *Dances with Wolves* (1992)

175.   *Soldier Blue* (1970)

176.   *Distant Drums* (1951)

177.   *I Will Fight No More Forever* (1975)

178.   *The Vanishing American* (1925)

179.   *Devil's Doorway* (1950)

180.   *The Naked Spur* (1953)

19. COMEDY WESTERNS

181. Who starred as "Painless" Potter in 1948?

182. Which comedy team followed Horace Greely's advice to *Go West* in 1941?

183. The Dirty Shame saloon was in which comedy/western?

184. *McLintock* (1963) is a western variation of which Shakespeare play?

185. Who was "the fastest finger in the west?"

186. In *Son of Paleface* (1952), which equine co-star shares a bed with Bob Hope?

187. In a running gag in 1974's *Blazing Saddles*, what is the surname of almost every resident of Rock Ridge?

188. Can you remember the name of the town in which Laurel and Hardy create mayhem in *Way Out West* in 1937?

189. In *The Sheepman* (1958), how does Jason Sweet provoke Jumbo into a fight?

190. Can you name the actor who starred as *Evil Roy Slade* in 1972?

20. TELEVISION WESTERNS 2

191.   What was the name of the ranch in *Bonanza?*

192.   In *Alias Smith and Jones* what were the main characters' alias Christian names?

193.   Following on from the previous question, who was Kid Curry and who was Hannibal Heyes?

194.   Who played the part of Sheriff Matt Dillon in *Gunsmoke?*

195.   Can you remember the name of the western series that starred a young Barbara Hershey as the elder sister of a family of orphans?

196.   In *Bonanza*, what was Hoss Cartwright's real Christian name, and who played him?

197.   What was the name of the town in which *The Virginian* was set?

198.   What was the name of Tonto's horse in *The Lone Ranger?*

199.   And, can you name the actor who became famous as the Lone Ranger?

200.   Who starred as Caine in *Kung Fu?*

21. DUKE'S LADIES

Can you name John Wayne's leading ladies in these westerns?

201. *The Big Trail* (1930)

202. *Tall in the Saddle* (1944)

203. *Angel and the Badman* (1947)

204. *The Fighting Kentuckian* (1949)

205. *Rio Grande* (1950)

206. *Hondo* (1953)

207. *Rio Bravo* (1959)

208. *North to Alaska* (1960)

209. *Rooster Cogburn* (1975)

210. *The Shootist* (1976)

22. WESTERN ICONS: RANDOLPH SCOTT

211. Randolph Scott was born in which U.S. state?

212. True or False? Randolph Scott played Hawkeye in the 1936 production of *The Last of the Mohicans*.

213. In which western does Randy play a character called Ben Brigade?

214. How many westerns did Budd Boetticher make with Randolph Scott?

215. What was the name of the town Randy found himself in all sorts of trouble in the 1958 oater *Buchanan Rides Alone*?

216. Which famous event did Randy's 1956 western *Seventh Calvary* revolve around?

217. Which duo had a hit single in 1973 with "Whatever happened to Randolph Scott?"

218. Which western was Randolph Scott's final movie?

219. Can you name the horse opera in which Randy teamed up with a pre-stardom James Garner?

220. In which year did Randolph Scott die?

23. MORE BAD GUYS

Can you remember who played these bad guys, and in which movies?

221.   Hedley Lamarr

222.   Charlie Wade

223.   Calvera

224.   Vic Hansbro

225.   Pesh–Chidin/El Brujo

226.   Rufus Ryker

227.   Jason Brett

228.   Waco Johnny Dean

229.   Denton Baxter

230.   Anton Chigurh

24. WESTERN SIDEKICKS

Can you name the actors who played the lead characters' loyal and sometimes comic friend in these westerns?

231.   Groot in *Red River* (1948)

232.   High Spade Frankie Wilson in *Winchester '73* (1950)

233.   Art Croft in *The Oxbow Incident* (1943)

234.   Willie Paine in *The Fighting Kentuckian* (1949)

235.   Bull Harris in *El Dorado* (1966)

236.   Deputy Billy Burns in *Trail Street* (1947)

237.   Jug May in *Support Your Local Gunfighter* (1971)

238.   Drago in *McLintock!* (1963)

239.   Rusty Hart in *Dodge City* (1939)

240.   California Carlson in *Three Men from Texas* (1940)

25. WHO ARE THOSE GUYS?

Can you name the actors who played these characters and also the movies they appeared in?

241. Pike Bishop

242. Martin Pawley

243. Henry Mendez

244. Steve Judd

245. Colonel Owen Thursday

246. Martin Brady

247. Glyn McLyntock

248. Gay Langland

249. Ben Train

250. John H. Mallory

26. MORE WESTERN QUOTES

From which westerns do the following quotes come from?

251. "I got no problem with killin' Boss..... never have."

252. "You gonna do something or stand there and bleed?"

253. "Why, when you've killed a man, why try to read the Lord in as a partner on the job?"

254. "If he'd just pay me what he's paying them to stop me from robbing him, I'd stop robbing him!"

255. "Hi Curly, kill anyone today?"

256. "I ain't spittin' on my whole life."

257. "A gun is as good or as bad as the man using it."

258. "Never rode shotgun on a hearse before."

259. "People scare better when they're dying."

260. "Hello handsome, is that a ten gallon hat or are you just enjoying the show?"

27. DUKE'S ROLES

Can you name the movies in which John Wayne played these characters?

261.   Thomas Dunson

262.   Captain Nathan Brittles

263.   Lieutenant Colonel Kirby Yorke

264.   Jake Cutter

265.   Colonel Cord McNally

266.   Cole Thornton

267.   Robert Marmaduke Hightower

268.   Taw Jackson

269.   Quirt Evans

270.   Bob Seton

28. WESTERN TRIVIA 3

271.   In which western did Marlon Brando wear a dress?

272.   Ted Cassidy appeared in *Butch Cassidy and The Sundance Kid*, but he was better known for his role in a famous television comedy series. Can you name the programme and the part Ted played?

273.   In the television series *MASH*, what was Colonel Potter's favourite movie?

274.   Can you name the Errol Flynn movie that inspired the name of an American country rock band?

275.   What was the name of Kirk Douglas's character's horse in *Lonely are the Brave* (1962)?

276.   Can you name the actor, more famous as a television detective, who originally played *Gunsmoke's* Matt Dillon on radio?

277.   William J. Lepetomane was a character in which comedy western, and who played him?

278.   *Five Guns West* (1955) was the directing debut of which maverick producer/director?

279. What is the name of the town in the 1964 Czech comedy/ western *Lemonade Joe*?

280. In 1965's *Cat Ballou*, John Marley played Cat Ballou's father, but in which famous non-western movie did he have some trouble with a horse?

29. LAWMEN

Can you name the actors who played these lawmen and, for an extra point, the movies?

281. Marshal Frank Patch

282. Sheriff Chris Hamish

283. Sheriff John T Chance

284. Sheriff Cobb

285. Sheriff Sam Deeds

286. Sheriff JP Harrah

287. Sheriff John T Langston

288. Marshal Jared Maddox

289. Marshal Clay Blaisdell

290. Marshal Matt Morgan

30. CLASSIC WESTERNS

291. Which cast member had top billing in the 1939 version of *Stagecoach*?

292. Which South American country did Butch and Sundance escape to in *Butch Cassidy and the Sundance Kid*?

293. Can you name the classic western that was based on a short story called *The Tin Star*?

294. How did Steve McQueen famously try to upstage Yul Brynner in *The Magnificent Seven*?

295. What did Brit in *The Magnificent Seven* and Mississippi in *El Dorado* have in common?

296. Which classic western was named the greatest western of all time by the American Film Institute in 2008?

297. Can you name the actor who played Will Kane's deputy in *High Noon*?

298. In John Ford's *Stagecoach*, how many of the passengers were killed by the Apaches?

299. What was Torrey's (played by Elisha J Cook) nickname in *Shane*?

300. How many Oscars did Clint Eastwood's *Unforgiven* win?

31. WESTERN ICONS: GARY COOPER

301. Gary Cooper was born in 1901 in which state: Montana, Missouri, or Michigan?

302. Coop was educated in England—true or false?

303. Can you name the 1929 western that made Coop a star?

304. Cooper won an Oscar in 1952 for his performance in *High Noon*. In which film did he win his first best actor Oscar?

305. Coop was unwell and couldn't attend the Oscar ceremony in 1953. Who accepted the best actor award for him?

306. Can you name the movie in which Coop played the head of a Quaker family during the civil war?

307. Can you name the Bob Hope movie in which Coop appeared in an uncredited cameo?

308. What was the title character's unusual Christian name in 1945's *Along Came Jones*?

309. Can you name the movie in which Coop played Wild Bill Hickok?

310. In which year did Gary Cooper die?

32. THE SILENTS

311. Can you name the 1903 silent short directed by Edwin Porter that is credited as giving birth to the western movie?

312. Can you name the famous director of *The Battle at Elderbush Gulch* (1914)?

313. Can you name the real-life train robber who starred in *The Bank Robbery* in 1910?

314. Who played the character Cheyenne Harry in several early western silents?

315. Who was the producer, writer, and director, known as "The Father of the Western" who died in suspicious circumstances in 1924?

316. Which Buster Keaton classic was based on a true incident in the American civil war?

317. Can you complete the title of this Tom Mix classic silent? *The Great K...........*

318. In John Ford's 1924 epic *The Iron Horse*, what was The Iron Horse?

319. *Tumbleweeds* (1925) told the story of a famous land rush. In which U.S. state did this occur?

320. *The Covered Wagon* (1923) established which great western movie cliché?

33. ALTERNATE TITLES

Can you match the movies with their alternate titles?

321. *From Hell to Texas* (1958)   *Killer on a Horse*

322. *Ride the High Country* (1962)   *Hollywood Cowboy*

323. *The Appaloosa* (1966)   *Rough Company*

324. *Along the Great Divide* (1951)   *The Trouble Shooter*

325. *Bend of the River* (1952)   *Manhunt*

326. *Welcome to Hard Times* (1966)   *Southwest to Sonora*

327. *Cheyenne* (1947)   *The Travellers*

328. *Hearts of the West* (1975)   *Guns in the Afternoon*

329. *The Violent Men* (1955)   *The Wyoming Kid*

330. *Man with the Gun* (1955)   *Where the River Bends*

34. SONGS

Can you identify the movies from these songs that featured in the films?

331. "Do Not Forsake Me"

332. "The Green Leaves of Summer"

333. "Blaze of Glory"

334. "Raindrops Keep Falling on My Head"

335. "Secret Love"

336. "Buttons and Bows"

337. "I Cain't Say No"

338. "A Four Legged Friend"

339. "Lonely Rider"

340. "My Rifle, My Pony and Me"

35. STATES

Can you name the U.S. States where these movies are set?

341.   *Lone Star* (1952)

342.   *Wichita* (1955)

343.   *Day of the Outlaw* (1959)

344.   *Virginia City* (1940)

345.   *The Unforgiven* (1960)

346.   *Bury My Heart at Wounded Knee* (2007)

347.   *Tell Them Willie Boy Is Here* (1969)

348.   *My Darling Clementine* (1946)

349.   *The Man from Laramie* (1955)

350.   *Abilene Town* (1946)

36. HORSES

Can you name the stars associated with these famous horses?

351. Starlight

352. Tony

353. Topper

354. Dollor

355. Fritz

356. Champion

357. Rush

358. Pie

359. Stardust

360. Buttermilk

37. THE 1930s

361. Who played *The Oklahoma Kid* in 1939?

362. Which other gangster star appeared in the above movie as a black-clad villain?

363. John Ford's *Drums along the Mohawk* (1939) was set during which war?

364. Walter Huston played "the killingest law officer who ever lived" in which 1932 western?

365. Who played Calamity Jane in 1936's *The Plainsman*?

366. Errol Flynn played Wade Hatton in 1939's *Dodge City*. Which real-life character was the basis for the character?

367. And can you name the director of *Dodge City*?

368. Who played a dual role in 1930's *River's End*?

369. What item of clothing does Boris Stavrogin (played by Mischa Auer) lose in a card game to Frenchy (Marlene Dietrich) in *Destry Rides Again* (1939)?

370. Which western won the best picture Oscar in 1931?

38. WESTERN ICONS: JAMES STEWART

371.   What was James Stewart's first western?

372.   In *Winchester '73* (1950), in which town did Jimmy's character win the prized rifle?

373.   In *Broken Arrow* (1950), which famous Apache chief did Jimmy's character become friends with?

374.   Jimmy starred in *The Rare Breed* in 1965. Who or what was "The Rare Breed?"

375.   What was Jimmy's profession in 1962's *The Man Who Shot Liberty Valance*?

376.   Who did Jimmy play in John Ford's *Cheyenne Autumn* in 1964?

377.   Who played Jimmy's brother in *Bandolero!* in 1968?

378.   Jimmy served during world war two in which branch of the services?

379.   What instrument did Jimmy play in *Night Passage* in 1957?

380.   In which year did James Stewart die?

39. TOWNS

Can you name the movies that were set in these fictional towns?

381. Hadleyville

382. Sawbuck Pass

383. Big Whiskey

384. Cayenne

385. Shinbone

386. Dime Box

387. Lago

388. Rock Ridge

389. Purgatory

390. Stodge City

40. COWBOYS

Can you name the actors who played these movie cowboys?

391. Monte Walsh in *Monte Walsh* (1970)

392. Tom Reese in *Cowboy* (1958)

393. Chuck Conner in *Saddle Tramp* (1950)

394. Doc Bender in *Cowboy* (1958)

395. Owen Daybright in *Vengeance Valley* (1951)

396. Lincoln Costain in *The Castaway Cowboy* (1972)

397. J.W. Coop in *J. W. Coop* (1971)

398. *Junior Bonner* (1972)

399. Matthew Garth in *Red River* (1948)

400. Monte Walsh in *Monte Walsh* (2003)

41. NAME THE MOVIE (PHOTO)

Can you identify the movie from the photograph?

401.

402.

403.

404.

405.

406.

407.

408.

409.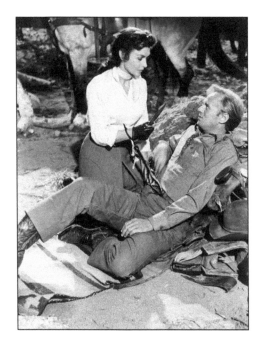

410.

42. THE OLDEST PROFESSION

Can you name the actresses who played these tarts with a heart?

411.   Dallas in *Stagecoach* (1939)

412.   Brandy in *Destry* (1954)

413.   Chihuahua in *My Darling Clementine* (1946)

414.   Kate Fisher in *Gunfight at the OK Corral* (1957)

415.   Hildy in *The Ballad of Cable Hogue* (1970)

416.   Constance Miller in *McCabe and Mrs Miller* (1971)

417.   Lily von Shtuup in *Blazing Saddles* (1974)

418.   Sara in *Two Mules for Sister Sara* (1970)

419.   Martine Bernard in *Monte Walsh* (1970)

420.   Agnes in *Butch Cassidy and the Sundance Kid* (1969)

43. THE GREAT WESTERN DIRECTORS: JOHN STURGES

421. Can you name the only western John Sturges made with Randolph Scott?

422. In *Bad Day at Black Rock* (1955), what was the name of the one-armed stranger played by Spencer Tracy?

423. What time does the train leave Gun Hill in *The Last Train from Gun Hill* (1959)?

424. In *The Magnificent Seven* (1960), how many of the seven were left alive at the end of the movie?

425. Who played the title role in Sturges's 1958 western *The Law and Jake Wade*?

426. *Hour of the Gun* (1967) told of events after which famous gunfight?

427. Which future Dynasty soap star was cast in *Escape from Fort Bravo* in 1953?

428. John Sturges directed Clint Eastwood in one western. Can you name it?

429. Who did Sturges cast as Wyatt Earp and Doc Holliday in 1957's *Gunfight at the OK Corral*?

430. Three of *The Magnificent Seven* cast appeared in *The Great Escape*, also directed by Sturges in 1963. Can you name them?

44. THE 1940s

431.   Who played George Armstrong Custer in *They Died with Their Boots On* in 1941?

432.   In the above movie, Custer had a fondness for eating which raw vegetable?

433.   Can you name the actors who played *The Three Godfathers* in 1948?

434.   Can you name the western that teamed Spencer Tracy with Katharine Hepburn in 1947?

435.   Can you name the actor who starred as *Whispering Smith* in 1949?

436.   What was the nickname of outlaw leader James Dawson (played by Gregory Peck) in 1948's *Yellow Sky*?

437.   Who was miscast as a Mexican outlaw in 1940's *Virginia City*?

438.   Can you name the 1946 western that features several Hoagy Carmichael songs?

439.   Can you name the former child star who in 1948, played Henry Fonda's daughter in *Fort Apache*?

440.   Which famous real-life western character did Robert Taylor play in 1941?

45. WESTERN ICONS: JOEL MCCREA

441. In which year was Joel McCrea born?

442. Which famous westerner did Joel McCrea play in a 1944 biopic?

443. What was the noteworthy and unusual feature of McCrea's 1948 oater *Four Faces West*?

444. Can you name the actress who Joel McCrea was married to for fifty-seven years?

445. In 1949's *South of St Louis*, how do McCrea's character and his two friends signify their bond?

446. What was unusual about McCrea's role and that of his co star Randolph Scott in *Ride the High Country*?

447. Can you name the actress who dedicated her Oscar to "her hero" Joel McCrea in 1981?

448. "I don't think God ever made a finer man than Joel McCrea." One of McCrea's co stars from *Ride the High Country* said this about him. Who was it?

449. Which real-life figure did McCrea play in *The First Texan* in 1956?

450. What was Joel McCrea's last movie?

46. GUNFIGHTERS

Name the actors who played these fictional gunfighters and the movies in which they appeared.

451. Jacob Wade

452. Clint Tollinger

453. Swifty Morgan

454. George Kelby Jr. aka George Temple

455. Bad Bob

456. Nelse McLeod

457. John Bernard Books

458. Nathan D Champion

459. Jules Gaspard d'Estaing

460. Cliff Hudspeth

47. SOLDIERS

Can you name the actors who played these real-life soldiers in the movies?

461. Major Robert Rogers in *Northwest Passage* (1940)

462. General Winfield Scott in *They Died with their Boots On* (1941)

463. Brigadier General George Crook in *Geronimo an American Legend* (1993)

464. Lieutenant General James Longstreet in *Gettysburg* (1993)

465. General Robert E Lee in *Gettysburg* (1993)

466. Jeb Stuart in *Santa Fe Trail* (1940)

467. Lieutenant General Phil Sheridan in *Rio Grande* (1950)

468. General Ulysses S Grant in *How the West Was Won* (1962)

469. General William Tecumseh Sherman in *How the West Was Won* (1962)

470. General George Armstrong Custer in *Custer of the West* (1967)

48. EARLY WESTERN STARS

471. Who was the stage-trained thespian who became a famous western star of the silent era in movies such as 1916's *Hells Hinges*?

472. Following on from the previous question, what was Hells Hinges?

473. Who did John Ford describe as the bright star of the early western sky?

474. Can you name the comedy genius who followed Horace Greely's advice to *Go West* in 1925?

475. Which star of western silent movies and "B" westerns was pictured on the cover of The Beatles' *Sergeant Pepper's Lonely Hearts Club Band Album*?

476. This early western star was a champion rodeo rider and worked with John Ford and Harry Carey. A star of silents and serials, he died in 1962.

477. Can you name the early western star who played the title roles in *The Squaw Man* and *The Virginian* in 1914?

478. Who played the title role in *The Vanishing American* in 1925?

479.   Can you name the bit-part player in *The Great Train
        Robbery* (1903) who made over 300 films and is considered
        the first great western movie star? He was awarded an
        honorary Oscar in 1957 for his role as a motion picture
        pioneer and for his contributions to the development of
        motion pictures as entertainment.

480.   This early western star was a cowboy, soldier, and stuntman
        before becoming a big star in "B" westerns. He died
        tragically in a fire in 1942.

49. GREAT BAD GUYS

481.   What despicable act did Jack Elam commit in *Rawhide* (1951)?

482.   I played Marshal Dan Troop on television and was a memorable villain in *Rio Bravo* and *Pale Rider*. Who am I?

483.   Who really did shoot Liberty Valance (Lee Marvin) in the 1962 classic?

484.   Who played Jesse James's assassin Bob Ford in *Jesse James* in 1939?

485.   Can you name the three actors who played Frank Miller's accomplices in *High Noon*?

486.   How is Justice Ellis McQueen Junior better known?

487.   What creature torments Jack Elam in the opening scenes of *Once Upon a Time in the West*?

488.   Richard Boone was a memorable bad guy in many westerns but played good guys too, particularly in television. Can you remember the lawman he played in a 1970s television series?

489.   Can you name the actor who forces Britt into the gun v. knife duel in *The Magnificent Seven*?

490.   Who played Tuco in *The Good, The Bad and The Ugly*?

50. SPAGHETTI WESTERNS 1

Can you translate the original Italian titles into their better-known English equivalents?

491. *C'era una volt ail west*

492. *Per un pugno di dollar*

493. *Per qualche dollaro in piu*

494. *Il buono, il brutto, il cattivo*

495. *Il grande silenzi*

496. *Lo chiamavano Trinità*

497. *Il mio nome è Nessuno*

498. *Da uomo a oumo*

499. *Faccia a faccia*

500. *Una pistola per Ringo*

51. THE BLUE AND THE GREY

501.   Can you name the author of the book on which the television miniseries *North and South* was based?

502.   In *Shenandoah* (1965), Charley Anderson's youngest son is wounded in battle. What happens next?

503.   Who played the Union scout in *Major Dundee* (1965)?

504.   Can you name the director of *Ride with the Devil* (1999)?

505.   In *Cold Mountain* (2003), a flock of birds appear in a vision of Inman to Ada. What type of bird?

506.   A young Harrison Ford featured in this 1968 civil war western with James Caan.

507.   Who directed the civil war sequence in *How the West Was Won* (1962)?

508.   Name the civil war drama based on real events in which Van Heflin plays a Confederate Major?

509.   Name the western that opens with the lead character firing the last shot of the civil war.

510.   In *Great Day in the Morning* (1956), what does Owen Pentecost played by Robert Stack win in a card game?

52. RACISM

511. Who played the title role in *Sergeant Rutledge* in 1960?

512. In *The Searchers*, what action does Ethan Edwards take when the search party finds a dead Comanche?

513. Who played the racist Cash in John Huston's *Unforgiven* (1960)?

514. Can you name the western starring Elvis Presley in which he played a half-breed shunned by white society?

515. In *Hombre* (1967) how do Paul Newman's fellow stage-coach passengers react when they discover he has been raised by Apaches?

516. In what circumstances do Chris and Vin team up at the start of *The Magnificent Seven*?

517. What is the guilty secret that the one-armed stranger uncovers in 1955's *Bad Day at Black Rock*?

518. In *The Halliday Brand* (1957), how does Big Dan Halliday react when he learns that his daughter loves a half-breed?

519. What incident sparks the manhunt for Chato in 1972's *Chato's Land*?

520. Name the movie in which the lead character says "One less buffalo means one less Indian."

53. SHOOT-OUTS

521. In *Stagecoach* (1939), what is Luke Plummer's card hand just before he faces The Ringo Kid in a shoot-out?

522. In *The Spikes Gang* (1974), which member of the gang kills Harry Spike in the tragic climax?

523. Can you name the legendary musician who faced Kirk Douglas in 1971's *A Gunfight*?

524. Name the three actors who face John Wayne in The Duke's final gunfight in *The Shootist*. (1976)

525. In *Warlock* (1959), Henry Fonda kills his best friend in a shoot-out. Who played his friend?

526. After the climatic gun fight in *High Noon*, what does Will Kane do with his marshal's badge?

527. What does Shane say to Jack Wilson prior to their climatic gunfight in *Shane* (1953)?

528. In *Vera Cruz* (1954), Gary Cooper and Burt Lancaster face each other in a shoot-out, both firing at the same time. What happens next?

529. Audrey Totter and Joan Leslie had a rare all-female gun duel in which Allan Dwan western?

530. What action sparks the climatic shoot out in *The Wild Bunch* (1969)?

54. WESTERN ICONS: BARBARA STANWYCK

531. Name the movie in which Barbara Stanwyck played a 109-year-old woman looking back on her life in the west.

532. Name the western television series in which Barbara played Victoria Barkley.

533. What was Barbara Stanwyck's real name?

534. In *The Furies* (1950), what was The Furies?

535. Name the western in which future President Ronald Reagan starred with Barbara.

536. "I was born upset," Barbara says in which western?

537. Can you name the Stanwyck western in which she is romanced by the Sundance Kid?

538. How is Barbara's character described in the theme song to *Forty Guns* (1957)?

539. Can you name the 1957 western in which Barbara teamed up with western great Joel McCrea?

540. In *The Violent Men* (1955), how does Barbara's character attempt to kill her husband?

55. CATCHPHRASES

Name the actor and the movie that made these catchphrases famous.

541.   "That'll be the day!"

542.   "Who are those guys?"

543.   "Not hardly."

544.   "Prove it."

545.   "You can't have no idea how little I care."

546.   "I had a friend once......."

547.   "Yoohoo, I'll make you famous!"

548.   "It is a good day to die."

549.   "Never should have left the Mississippi!"

550.   "Never apologize Mister, it's a sign of weakness."

56. MORE WESTERN OSCARS

551. Can you name the two actors who won Oscars for their performance in *Hud* (1963)?

552. How many Oscar nominations did the Coen Brothers' *True Grit* (2010) receive?

553. How many Oscars did *Butch Cassidy and the Sundance Kid* win?

554. Who won the Oscar for best song for *High Noon* (1952)?

555. *Shane* (1953) won only one Oscar. In which category?

556. For which John Ford western did Winston C Hoch win the best cinematography Oscar?

557. Who won the best director Oscar for *Dances with Wolves* (1990)?

558. Who won an Oscar for his performance in *Glory* in 1989?

559. Who won an Oscar for cinematography for *Hud* in 1963?

560. The *Alamo* (1960) won only one Oscar. In which category?

57. REMAKES

561. Who played the Ringo Kid in the 1966 remake of *Stagecoach*?

562. *The Shakiest Gun in the West* (1968) was a remake of which classic comedy western?

563. *The Badlanders* (1958) was a remake of which seminal crime drama?

564. In 1981, *High Noon* was remade with an outer space location. What was the movie?

565. *Sergeants Three* (1963) was a rat pack remake of which classic George Stevens movie?

566. Name the actor who took the John Wayne role in the 1988 television remake of *Red River*.

567. Who took the James Stewart role in the 1967 remake of *Winchester '73*?

568. *The Magnificent Seven* was a remake of which famous Japanese movie?

569. *The Outrage* (1964) was a remake of the Japanese classic *Rashomen*. Who starred as the Mexican bandit in *The Outrage*?

570. *House of Strangers* (1949) was remade in 1954 by Edward Dymtryk. What was it called?

58. THE 1950s

571. 1956's *Tension at Table Rock* featured a young actress in an early role who would make a big impression three years later in the role of "Feathers." Name the actress and the movie in which she played "Feathers."

572. In 1957, which future Star Trek star played Morgan Earp in *Gunfight at the OK Corral*?

573. What was notable about the trio of 1953 westerns *Hondo, The Charge at Feather River*, and *Gun Fury*?

574. What does Bob Hope call the two vultures who hitch a ride on his jalopy in *Son of Paleface* (1952)?

575. What weapon does Walter Matthau use against Burt Lancaster in 1955's *The Kentuckian*?

576. In 1955, Ray Milland directed his first movie, a western. What was it?

577. Which real-life outlaw did Rock Hudson play in *The Lawless Breed* (1953)?

578. Who directed *Apache* in 1954?

579. Rod Steiger starred in *The Run of the Arrow* in 1956. What was the run of the arrow?

580. Where was Robert Parrish's *The Wonderful Country* (1959)?

59. THE GREAT WESTERN DIRECTORS: BUDD BOETTICHER

581. Budd Boetticher was a bullfighter before he entered the movie industry—true or false?

582. What did critic Andrew Sarris call Boetticher's series of westerns with Randolph Scott?

583. Who was the screenwriter, later to become a notable western director himself, who worked with Boetticher on many of the Randolph Scott westerns?

584. Boetticher's *The Tall T* is based on a short story by which famous crime novelist?

585. Can you name the Clint Eastwood western based on a Budd Boetticher story?

586. What symbolic action does Randolph Scott's character take at the climax of *Ride Lonesome* (1959)?

587. Name the actors who played the two brothers in Boetticher's *Horizons West* (1952).

588. Who did Boetticher call "the toughest guy in the movie business?"

589. Which Boetticher western featured Lee Marvin in an early role as the villainous Bill Masters?

590. Which western icon produced a documentary on Budd Boetticher in 2005?

60. WESTERN ICONS: HENRY FONDA

591. In which year was Henry Fonda born?

592. Fonda worked with John Ford for the first time in 1939 in two movies. Name them.

593. Henry Fonda's son Peter, directed and starred in a 1971 western. Can you name it?

594. Henry Fonda's portrayal of an embittered martinet colonel in *Fort Apache* (1948) had parallels with which real-life character?

595. In 1968's *Once Upon a Time in the West*, Fonda gained infamy with one shocking act at the start of the movie. What did his character do?

596. Can you name the western movie in which Fonda's character fakes a heart attack?

597. In *My Darling Clementine*, Wyatt Earp (Fonda) has only one simple ambition in his first night in Tombstone. What is it?

598. Fonda teamed up with Glenn Ford as two cowboys in a light hearted oater from 1964. What was the movie?

599. Can you name the two westerns in which Fonda starred with his great friend James Stewart in the twilight of their careers?

600. Can you name the western which climaxes with Fonda's character reading an emotional letter?

61. UNSUNG

Can you name the singers and musicians who starred in these westerns?

601.   *Rio Bravo* (1959)

602.   *North to Alaska* (1960)

603.   *The Alamo* (1960)

604.   *The Fastest Guitar Alive* (1967)

605.   *True Grit* (1969)

606.   *Gunfight in Abilene* (1967)

607.   *The Electric Horseman* (1979)

608.   *Dead Man* (1995)

609.   *Ride with the Devil* (1999)

610.   *Comanche* (2000)

62. GREAT WESTERN BAD GUYS (PHOTO)

Who are these memorable western bad guys?

611.

Name both actors

612.

613.

614.

615.

616.

617.

618.

619.

620.

63. THEY TURNED IT DOWN

621. What part in *Butch Cassidy and the Sundance Kid* did Jack Lemmon turn down?

622. Can you name the English-born actor who turned down the role of Cherry Valance in *Red River*?

623. Which Oscar-winning star turned down the role of Pike Bishop in *The Wild Bunch*?

624. Name the actor who was reputed to have turned down roles in *Shane, Rio Bravo,* and *High Noon.*

625. Which actor turned down the role of English Bob in *Unforgiven* because he felt he was too young for the part?

626. Can you name the great western character actor who turned down the role of Jack Wilson in *Shane* because he didn't think he had enough lines?

627. Prior to John Wayne taking the part, who turned down the title role in *Hondo*?

628. Marlon Brando, Gregory Peck, Charlton Heston, and John Wayne all turned down the same role. Which one?

629. Kirk Douglas turned down which role made famous by Lee Marvin?

630. James Stewart turned down which role in *The Wild Bunch*?

64. NAME THE MOVIE (CAST)

Can you identify the western from the members of the cast?

631. Henry Fonda, Anthony Quinn, Richard Widmark.

632. Kirk Douglas, Robert Mitchum, Richard Widmark.

633. Marlon Brando, Karl Malden, Ben Johnson.

634. Clark Gable, Marilyn Monroe, Montgomery Clift.

635. Paul Newman, Frederic March, Richard Boone.

636. William Holden, Ryan O'Neal, Karl Malden.

637. Clark Gable, Jane Russell, Robert Ryan

638. Ed Harris, Viggo Mortenson, Jeremy Irons.

639. James Garner, Sidney Poitier, Dennis Weaver.

640. Gregory Peck, Stephen Boyd, Henry Silva.

65. THE 1960s

641. Can you name the four actors who played *The Professionals* in 1966?

642. Who did Marlon Brando replace as director of *One Eyed Jacks* (1961)?

643. Clark Gable made his last movie in 1961. What was it?

644. What was the revolutionary filming process used in *How the West Was Won* (1962)?

645. What was unusual about Tim Strawn's appearance (Lee Marvin) in 1965's *Cat Ballou*?

646. Who starred as Sam Whiskey in 1967?

647. Who won the Oscar for his screenplay in *Butch Cassidy and the Sundance Kid* (1969)?

648. Can you name the western that begins with the United Artists logo being ripped apart by a bloody knife?

649. Can you name the cowpoke who was "damn near fifty years old" and, "Too soon old, too late smart?"

650. In *Support Your Local Sheriff!* (1969) what country was Jason McCullough, (played by James Garner) travelling to?

66. "B" WESTERNS

651. Which husband and wife were known as the King of the Cowboys and the Queen of the West?

652. What role did John Wayne play in *The Three Mesquiteers* series?

653. Why was Lash La Rue so called?

654. Can you name the star of "B" westerns who also played Tarzan, Buck Rogers, and Flash Gordon?

655. What was the name of Roy Rogers's dog?

656. Who played Hopalong Cassidy from 1935 until 1954?

657. Which singing cowboy had hits with "Silver Haired Daddy of Mine" and "Back in the Saddle Again?"

658. Which "B" movie star's trademark was a pair of six-guns worn butt forward in their holsters?

659. Who played Windy Halliday, and whose sidekick was he?

660. Who played Singing Sandy?

67. THE GREAT WESTERN DIRECTORS: JOHN FORD

661. True or false? John Ford was born in Ireland.

662. Can you name Ford's brother who was also an actor and director?

663. "When the truth becomes the legend, print the legend," is a famous line from which John Ford western?

664. How many Oscars did *The Searchers* (1956) win?

665. In *Rio Grande* (1950), what crime does Mrs. Yorke (Maureen O'Hara) accuseQuincannon (Victor McLaglen) of?

666. What was John Ford's real name?

667. What rank did John Ford achieve in the United States Navy?

668. Can you name the famous director who, when asked which directors he most admired, replied, "The old masters. By which I mean John Ford, John Ford, and John Ford."

669. Ford adopted an unusual position to film the famous riverbank scene in 1961's *Two Road Together*. Where did he position himself to film the scene?

670. What was the Ford movie that featured a young John Wayne as an excited spectator of a horse race?

68. TAGLINES

Can you name the westerns that were promoted with the following taglines?

671. *She had the biggest six–shooters in the west!*

672. *There were three men in her life. One to take her... one to love her... and one to kill her.*

673. *An army of one.*

674. *For three men the civil war wasn't hell, it was practice!*

675. *He had to find her... he had to find her!*

676. *Together for the first time James Stewart and John Wayne.*

677. *When the hands point up... the excitement starts!*

678. *Not that it matters but most of it is true.*

679. *Nine men who came too late and stayed too long.*

680. *Love is a force of nature.*

69. STUDIOS

Can you match the studios with these classic westerns?

681. MGM   *The Magnificent Seven* (1960)

682. Miramax   *Shane* (1953)

683. RKO   *Dead Man* (1995)

684. Republic   *Destry Rides Again* (1939)

685. Warner Brothers   *Comanche Station* (1960)

686. Universal   *The Ox-Bow Incident* (1943)

687. Columbia   *Rio Grande* (1950)

688. United Artists   *Unforgiven* (1992)

689. Paramount   *Fort Apache* (1948)

690. Twentieth Century Fox   *The Naked Spur* (1953)

70. REAL LIFE

Can you name the actors who played these real-life western characters?

691.   Brigham Young in *Brigham Young – Frontiersman* (1940)

692.   Belle Starr in *The Long Riders* (1980)

693.   Judge Roy Bean in *The Westerner* (1940)

694.   William Quantrill in *Dark Command* (1940)

695.   Bat Masterton in *Gunfight at the OK Corral* (1957)

696.   Billy the Kid in *The Left Handed Gun* (1958)

697.   Buffalo Bill (William Cody) in *Buffalo Bill and the Indians* (1976)

698.   Doc Holliday in *My Darling Clementine* (1946)

699.   Sam Houston in *The Alamo* (2004)

700.   John Brown in *Santa Fe Trail* (1940)

71. CATTLE BARONS

These actors played cattle barons in westerns. Can you match the actor with the movie?

701. Donald Crisp   *The Rare Breed* (1966)

702. Ed Asner   *Forty Guns* (1957)

703. Spencer Tracey   *Duel in the Sun* (1946)

704. Jason Robards   *The Furies* (1957)

705. Jeannie Crain   *The Man from Laramie* (1955)

706. Barbara Stanwyck   *The Culpepper Cattle Company* (1972)

707. Walter Huston   *Broken Lance* (1954)

708. Brian Keith   *Comes a Horseman* (1978)

709. Billy Green Bush   *Man Without a Star* (1955)

710. Lionel Barrymore   *El Dorado* (1966)

72. THE GREAT WESTERN DIRECTORS: SERGIO LEONE

711.   James Coburn and Charles Bronson both turned down the lead role in which Sergio Leone western?

712.   Leone was the assistant director of which multiple-Oscar-winning Hollywood epic of the 1950s?

713.   *A Fistful of Dollars* (1964) was a remake of which Japanese film?

714.   In which country was the so called "Dollars trilogy" largely filmed?

715.   How do Blondie and Tuco first meet in *The Good, the Bad and the Ugly*?

716.   How does Clint Eastwood's character cheat death in *A Fistful of Dollars*?

717.   In which iconic western movie location was much of *Once Upon a Time in the West* filmed (1968)?

718.   Where does the climatic shoot out in *The Good, the Bad, and the Ugly* take place?

719.   Who was Leone's frequent musical collaborator?

720.   From which Leone movie does this quote come from? "Now that you've called me by name. . . ."

73. FEMME FATALES

Femme fatales are traditionally found in film noir, but the western has its fair share. Can you identify the actresses who played these roles?

721.   Vienna in *Johnny Guitar* (1954)

722.   Mae Horgan in *Jubal* (1956)

723.   Connie Dickason in *Ramrod* (1947)

724.   Alice Williams in *The Bounty Hunter* (1954)

725.   Altar Keane in *Rancho Notorious* (1952)

726.   Pearl Chavez in *Duel in the Sun* (1946)

727.   Kate Quantrill/Kitty McCoy in *Woman They Almost Lynched* (1953)

728.   Countess Marie Duvarre in *Vera Cruz* (1954)

729.   Lily Dollar in *Warlock* (1959)

730.   Lucy Overmire in *Canyon Passage* (1946)

74. WESTERN STALWARTS 1

731.   Can you name the western stalwart who made more than forty westerns, beginning with 1930's *The Big Trail* and ending with *Rio Bravo* in 1959?

732.   Which actor, born in 1916, was reputed to be one of the fastest draws in Hollywood?

733.   Can you name the western stalwart who was a circus acrobat prior to becoming an actor?

734.   I was born in 1928 and made my name on television as a charming con man and gambler. I also made several western movies before returning to television as a famous private eye. Who am I?

735.   Can you name the veteran stuntman born in 1920, who doubled for numerous stars such as Roy Rogers and Gary Cooper, before becoming an actor who was Oscar nominated in a 1978 western?

736.   Which actor featured in both *My Darling Clementine* and *Gunfight at the OK Corral*?

737.   Her real name was Joanne Letitia LaCock and she was married to the actor in question 736—How is she better known?

738.   1969 was a good year for western stalwart Jeff Corey. He appeared in two of the most loved westerns of all time. Can you name them?

739.   Whose facial hair caused some controversy in a 1950s western?

740.   I was born in 1909 and made my name playing villains in film noir, and then westerns. I played a particularly mean Sundance Kid in 1948. Who am I?

75. WESTERN ICONS:
BEN JOHNSON

Ben Johnson was a real cowboy, and was therefore a realistic, comforting presence in many western movies. Can you name the films in which he played these characters?

741. Travis Blue

742. Tector Gorch

743. Short Grubb

744. James Pepper

745. Chris Calloway

746. Mister

747. Sergeant Chillum

748. Sergeant Tyree

749. Bob Amory

750. Trooper Tyree

76. THE 1970s

751. Which western took most money at the U.S. box office in the 1970s?

752. Which gang of outlaws featured in 1971's *The Great Northfield Minnesota Raid*?

753. Can you name the 1970s western about a long-distance horse race?

754. The son of a great western character actor composed the soundtrack for *Jeremiah Johnson*. Who was he and who was his father?

755. Can you name the Scottish screenwriter of 1970s westerns *Ulzana's Raid* and *Billy Two Hats*?

756. Name the two actors who played the title characters in 1979's *Butch and Sundance: The Early Days*.

757. Who played a *Man Called Sledge* in 1970?

758. Can you name the western directed by Kirk Douglas in 1975?

759. One of the *Long Riders* cast won an Oscar for best song in 1976. Can you name him?

760. Can you name the 1978 western starring and directed by Jack Nicholson?

77. BURT AND KIRK

Burt Lancaster and Kirk Douglas were great friends on and off screen. Their movie roles, especially in westerns, were very similar. But who played these roles, Burt or Kirk? For an extra point, name the movies too.

761.   Joe Erin

762.   William J Tadlock

763.   Howard Nightingale

764.   Colonel Thaddeus Gearhart

765.   John W Burns

766.   Brendan O'Mally

767.   Joe Bass

768.   Archie McIntosh

769.   Dempsey Rae

770.   Bill Dolworth

78. THE GREAT WESTERN DIRECTORS: SAM PECKINPAH

771. Name the first western movie directed by Sam Peckinpah.

772. Can you recall the television western series that Peckinpah helped to develop and also produced, wrote, and directed?

773. Can you name the movie in which Peckinpah's name is engraved on a tombstone?

774. Who threatened to run Peckinpah through with a sabre on the set of *Major Dundee*?

775. Early in his career, Peckinpah worked as assistant director to a director who would be a huge influence on Clint Eastwood. Name the director.

776. Can you name the 1965 western that Peckinpah scripted but did not direct?

777. Can you name the Peckinpah western in which a character asks his brother, "Ain't you got no sense of family honour?"

778. "This time we do it right," is a line from which Peckinpah western?

779. Just before his death, Peckinpah filmed music videos for which musician and singer?

780. Which actor modelled an Oscar-winning performance on Sam Peckinpah?

79. WESTERN STALWARTS 2

781.   Can you name the son of an Oscar-winning star of John Ford's stock company who directed many westerns in the 1960s and 1970s?

782.   Who played the title role in the 1959 western *The Hangman*?

783.   MacDonald Carey, Alan Ladd, Sterling Hayden, Richard Widmark, and Jason Patric all played which legendary western adventurer?

784.   Can you name the western stalwart of the past forty years who was memorably described by film critic Philip French as the natural successor as life's fall-guy to Elisha J Cook Jr?

785.   Who starred as Rooster Coburn in the 1978 television version of *True Grit*?

786.   How many Oscars did the great western stalwart Walter Brennan win?

787.   *Gunsmoke* star James Arness had a brother who was also an actor. Can you name him?

788.   On the same theme, who was Dana Andrews's actor brother?

789.   Who played the "little squirt" who forces Jimmy Ringo to draw in the opening scenes of *The Gunfighter* (1950)?

790.   Who made his movie debut as Whit in 1959's *Ride Lonesome*?

80. MUSICAL WESTERNS

Can you recall the musical westerns that featured these songs?

791. "I Talk to the Trees"

792. "On The Atchison, Topeka, and the Santa Fe"

793. "Bless Your Beautiful Hide"

794. "The Surrey With the Fringe On Top"

795. "Anything You Can Do"

796. "Just Blew In From The Windy City"

797. "Clementine Capers"

798. "A Dime and a Dollar"

799. "The Girl That I Marry"

800. "They Call the Wind Maria"

81. KIDS

Can you name the actors who played these memorable roles in westerns?

801.   Little Joey in *Shane* (1953)

802.   Jeff Yorke in *Rio Grande* (1950)

803.   Dot Gilkeson in *The Missing* (2003)

804.   Mattie Ross in *True Grit* (2010)

805.   David Chandler in *The Proud Rebel* (1958)

806.   Megan Wheeler in *Pale Rider* (1985)

807.   Mark Calder in *The River of No Return* (1954)

808.   Johnny Allen in *Return of the Badmen* (1948)

809.   Slim Honeycutt in *The Cowboys* (1972)

810.   Horace Greeley Allen in *Will Penny* (1968)

82. DEATH IN THE WEST

811.   In *The Ballad of Cable Hogue* (1970), how does Cable Hogue die?

812.   In *Pat Garrett and Billy the Kid* (1973), what song is playing on the soundtrack as Sheriff Baker (Slim Pickens) dies by the river?

813.   In *Once Upon a Time in the West* (1968), what does Harmonica do in response to the dying Frank's question, "Who are you?"

814.   In *Ride the High Country* (1962), what are Steve Judd's last words to Gil Westrum before he dies?

815.   How did evil Charlie Gilson (played by Robert Taylor) die in *The Last Hunt* (1956)?

816.   Can you name the actor who gained infamy by killing John Wayne's character in *The Cowboys* (1972)?

817.   In Delmer Daves's *The Last Wagon* (1956), what implement does Comanche Todd use to kill his captor?

818.   Can you name the three actors who played the three innocent men who were lynched in *The Ox-Bow Incident* (1943)?

819.   What were Gus McCrae's last words to Woodrow Call in *Lonesome Dove* (1989)?

820.   How does Jimmy Ringo meet his death in *The Gunfighter* (1950)?

83. THE 1980s

821.   Name the film studio that was brought to its knees by the failure of *Heaven's Gate*.

822.   Which country-and-western legend played the title role in 1980's *Barbarosa*?

823.   Can you name the famous western that was remade for television in 1986 with a quartet of revered singers and musicians in the main roles?

824.   Which 1985 western did its director call "A western *Raiders of the Lost Ark*?"

825.   Can you name the 1989 film that told the true story of an African-American regiment during the American civil war?

826.   *Young Guns* (1988) and its follow up *Young Guns II* (1990) told the story of which legendary western figure?

827.   In 1980's *Tom Horn*, Horn (Steve McQueen) is beaten up by which real-life boxer?

828.   Who starred as *The Grey Fox* in 1982?

829.   Can you name the musicians who played the title roles in *The Last Days of Frank and Jesse James* in 1986?

830.   Which western genre did 1985's *Rustler's Rhapsody* spoof?

84. WESTERN ICONS: CLINT EASTWOOD

831. In which year was Clint born?

832. What was the name of Eastwood's character in the television series *Rawhide*?

833. In *High Plains Drifter* (1973) Eastwood's character renames the town of Lago as what?

834. How does Eastwood's character die in *The Beguiled* (1971)?

835. Can you name the director who made five movies with Clint, including three westerns?

836. What was the first western that Clint directed?

837. Which two directors did Clint dedicate *Unforgiven* (1992) to?

838. Can you name the town where Clint served as Mayor in the 1980s?

839. In *Bronco Billy* (1980), what was Bronco Billy's occupation before he formed his Wild West show?

840. Which Eastwood western has a gravestone with Sergio Leone's name on it?

85. THE GREAT WESTERN DIRECTORS: RAOUL WALSH

841. How were westerns such as Walsh's *Pursued* (1947) described?

842. What was the occupation of Kenneth More's character in Walsh's 1958 comedy western *The Sheriff of Fractured Jaw*?

843. Walsh directed one of the first talkie westerns. It featured the Cisco Kid. What was it?

844. Raoul Walsh began his movie career as an actor. Can you name the infamous real-life character who he played in *Birth of a Nation* (1915)?

845. Can you name the early John Wayne western that Walsh directed in 1930?

846. Walsh remade his classic gangster movie *High Sierra* as a western. What was the title?

847. Walsh's *Distant Drums* (1951) was set in which U.S. state?

848. What was Raoul Walsh's last western?

849. Which Walsh western was The Doors' Jim Morrison reputed to have watched on the night of his death?

850. In Walsh's *They Died with Their Boots On* (1941), which Sioux chief kills George Custer?

86. GREAT WESTERN CHARACTER ACTOR (PHOTO)

Can you identify these great western character actors?

851.

852.

853.

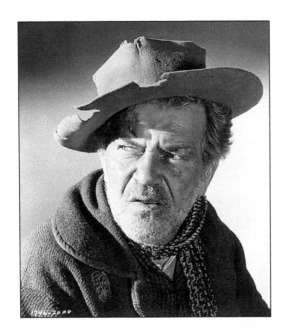

854.

855.

856.

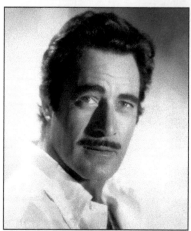

857.

858.

859.

860.

87. SPAGHETTI WESTERNS 2

861. Who described spaghetti westerns as "No stories, just killing?"

862. Which spaghetti-western director lamented the fact that while John Ford had John Wayne, and Sergio Leone had Clint Eastwood, he had Franco Nero?

863. Which major figure in spaghetti westerns did *Time Magazine* call a serious bore?

864. Can you name the spaghetti western in which a member of The Ku Klux Klan is forced to eat his own ear?

865. In *Shanghai Noon* (2000) there is a character whose name pays tribute to a great spaghetti-western star. What is the character's name?

866. Who played the title role in 1966's *Navajo Joe*?

867. "It is a very fine film, but it is my film." Akira Kurosawa said this about which spaghetti western?

868. Bob Robertson was the pseudonym of which major figure in the history of spaghetti westerns?

869. Can you name the spaghetti western in which the lead character carries a coffin with him wherever he goes?

870. And what does he carry in the coffin?

88. WESTERN ICONS: ROBERT MITCHUM

871. In which year was Mitchum born?

872. Mitchum initially made his name as a villain in a series of "B" westerns starring whom?

873. How did Mitchum describe his part in *Eldorado* (1966)?

874. Mitchum played Marshal Jim Flagg in which 1969 western?

875. What was the 1993 western that Mitchum narrated?

876. What songs does Mitchum sing in *Pursued* (1947)?

877. Mitchum appeared with Marilyn Monroe in one western. What was it called, and for an extra point who played Monroe's no-good husband?

878. Mitchum served three months in jail in 1948. What was his crime?

879. In which western did Mitchum shoot at his own real-life brother?

880. In *Five Card Stud* (1968), where did Mitchum's character conceal his revolver?

89. NATIVE AMERICANS 2

881.   In *Little Big Man* (1970), what tribe adopts Jack Crabb (played by Dustin Hoffman)?

882.   In *Jeremiah Johnson* (1972), Johnson leads a cavalry troop through burial grounds belonging to which tribe?

883.   In which movie does Cherokee Lone Watie say that his tribe is civilised because they are easy to sneak up on?

884.   What tribe does the villainous Magua belong to in the much filmed *The Last of the Mohicans*?

885.   In *A Man Called Horse* (1970), what ancient ritual does Richard Harris undergo?

886.   He was born Espera DeCorti in 1907, the son of Italian immigrants, but became better known when he changed his name. He lived and worked as an Indian, and appeared in many westerns over a period of sixty years. His fame allowed him to help many Native American charities. How was he better known?

887.   Who took the title role in *Tell Them Willie Boy Is Here* in 1969, and which famous Humphrey Bogart movie did he appear in as a child?

888.   *Last of the Dogmen* (1995) tells the story of the discovery of an unknown band of dog soldiers from which tribe?

889. Who played *Chief Crazy Horse* in the 1955 biopic?

890. In *White Feather* (1955) what is signified by a Cheyenne warrior throwing a knife, with a white feather attached, into the ground?

90. THE 1990s

891.   How are the gang known as "The Cowboys" identified in 1993's *Tombstone*?

892.   In *Tombstone*, what does Doc do in reply to some fancy gun twirling by Johnny Ringo?

893.   Name the rock star who composed the soundtrack to *Dead Man* in 1995?

894.   *Dances with Wolves* (1990) became the first western to win the best picture Oscar since which film?

895.   How many Oscars did *Dances with Wolves* win?

896.   In which iconic western location was *The High Lo Country* (1998) partly filmed?

897.   In *Back to the Future Part 3*, what name does Marty adopt in the wild west?

898.   How did Jack Palance celebrate his best supporting actor award at the 1992 Oscars?

899.   "I like westerns. I don't know what they have to do with anything, but I like them." Which 1990 movie does this quote come from?

900.   Who starred as *Conagher* in 1991?

91. STRANGE BUT TRUE

901. Tom Mix was a pall bearer at which real-life western legend's funeral?

902. What was the name of the character played by Dick Powell in 1951's *The Tall Target*, and whose assassination was he trying to prevent?

903. In *Support Your Local Sheriff* (1969), what is the unusual feature of the new jail?

904. In his song "Brownsville Girl" Bob Dylan sings about a famous actor in a classic western. Name the actor and movie.

905. Can you name the two actors that played father and son in *The Halliday Brand* (1957) despite being almost the same age?

906. In an unusual piece of casting, Dame Judith Anderson played an ancient Sioux in which 1970 western?

907. In *Ride the High Country* (1962), there is a race between a horse and an animal not usually associated with westerns. What kind of animal?

908. Mercedes Cambridge played a memorable role in *Johnny Guitar* in 1954, but she is probably best known for her work in which 1970s horror movie?

909. Can you name the James Stewart western that was turned into a musical?

910. In *Tombstone* (1993), the character of Billy Claiborne was played by a descendent of which famous historical figure?

92. THE GREAT WESTERN DIRECTORS: ANTHONY MANN

911.   True or false? Anthony Mann was born Emil Anton Bundesmann in Berlin in 1906.

912.   In *The Far Country* (1954) what does James Stewart's horse have on its saddle–horn?

913.   How many westerns did Mann make with James Stewart?

914.   What disfigurement does James Stewart's character in *Bend of the River* (1952) have?

915.   In *Man of the West* (1958), what do the gang discover when they reach the town of Lassoo intending to rob the bank?

916.   In *Bend of the River* (1952), how do James Stewart and Arthur Kennedy's character first meet?

917.   Bart Bogardus is a character in an Anthony Mann western. Can you name the movie and the screen heavy who played him?

918.   Which Mann/Stewart western was nominated for an Oscar for best screenplay?

919.   In *Bend of the River* (1952) what four words does James Stewart spit at Arthur Kennedy when he is beaten and left behind by the wagon train?

920.   What is Morg Hickman's (Henry Fonda) occupation in 1957's *The Tin Star*?

93. WESTERN STALWARTS 3

921. Who played the drunk who Marshal Will Kane released from his jail in *High Noon*?

922. Can you name the two actors who appeared in the original 1950 version of *Winchester '73* and the 1967 television remake?

923. What was character-actor Guinn Williams's nickname?

924. Who was John Ford's son-in-law who appeared in several of his westerns?

925. He worked as a producer on famed television series *Rawhide* in the 1950s before producing a number of low-budget westerns for Paramount such as *Buckskin* and *Waco*, and he also helped produce *Deadwood* for television. In all, he was associated with Paramount for eighty-five years until his death in 2013. Who was he?

926. Can you name the member of John Ford's stock company who invited Wyatt Earp and his "lady fair" to a "dag-blasted good dance?"

927. Who played the legendary Apache leader Cochise in three films in the 1950s?

928. What was the nickname of Harry Carey Junior?

929. Can you name the western stalwart who rode the "H" bomb in *Dr Strangelove* in 1963?

930. Victor McLaglen, the great character actor who starred in many John Ford westerns as an Irish Sergeant, was actually born in Tunbridge Wells, England. True or false?

94. FOREIGN DEPARTURES

The western is truly international with filmmakers around the world drawn to the genre. Can you rearrange the movie title with the countries that produced them?

931. *Utu* (1983)   France

932. *El Topo* (1966)   Canada

933. *Death Rides a Horse* (1968)   Great Britain

934. *The Treasure of Silver Lake* (1965)   India

935. *Tears of the Black Tiger* (2000)   Australia

936. *Viva Maria!* (1965)   New Zealand

937. *The Grey Fox* (1982)   Germany

938. *The Proposition* (2005)   Mexico

939. *The Sheriff of Fractured Jaw* (1958)   Italy

940. *Sholay* (1975)   Thailand

95. WESTERN TURKEYS

Can you name the less-than-great westerns from the description?

941. An all-star cast led by a Scottish cowboy failed to bring Louis L'Amour's novel to life.

942. This 1930s "B" western has a cast entirely of midgets.

943. A disaster from the usually reliable Burt Kennedy, starring one of the twentieth century's greatest singers. The title is cockney rhyming slang for three.

944. A legendary western gunman meets up with Transylvania's finest in William "One-Shot" Beaudine's exploitation pic.

945. This 1999 flop was a big screen adaption of a popular 1960s television series, but it did produce a hit record for its star.

946. The statuesque Ursula Andress and Anita Ekberg were the only memorable features of this rat pack outing.

947. In *Something Big* (1971) Dean Martin's horse has the only memorable feature in the film. What is it?

948. Elvis Presley grew a beard to star as a reformed gunfighter in this 1969 dud.

949. Sadly, this comic misfire will be remembered for the great John Candy's death during filming.

950. Described as the first electric western, this turkey featured a young Don Johnson and the James Gang. That's the '70s rock group, not the infamous outlaws.

96. NAME THAT KID

What would the western movie be like without the "Kid?" In some westerns he's the callow youth, in others the sharp shooting gunfighter. Can you remember the movies and, in one case, a television programme that featured these kids?

951.   The Soda Pop Kid

952.   The Utica Kid

953.   The Schofield Kid

954.   The Waco Kid

955.   The Rumpo Kid

956.   The Dancing Kid

957.   The Silver Kid

958.   The Halitosis Kid

959.   The Oregon Kid

960.   The Shanghai Kid

97. NAME THE MOVIE

Can you name the western movie from the plot?

961. After deserting his command, trooper Bart Lash assumes the identity of a dead cavalry officer to help a wagon train against marauding Indians.

962. A doctor with a past nurses a blind girl back to health but must confront his past and the villain who has his own designs on the girl.

963. Pat Garrett enlists Wyatt Earp and Bat Masterton for a showdown with Butch Cassidy's gang in Abilene.

964. When he insists on treating a malaria outbreak amongst Indians, a young army doctor at a remote Cavalry post is drawn into conflict with his racist commanding officer.

965. An army scout takes a white woman and her Apache son under his wing, but the boy's father is on their trail.

966. A deranged Confederate officer attempts to prolong the civil war by arming Apaches against the Union.

967. Two ageing gunfighters sell tickets for a winner-takes-all shoot-out.

968.   Wes Steele is suspected of robbing a stagecoach and killing the occupants, and he must prove that the real villains are the local banker and sheriff.

969.   An ageing marshal is forcibly retired and must team up with his one-time adversary to stop the bad guys robbing a train.

970.   In this noir western, a drifting gunslinger with a conscience is hired by a cattle rustler to intimidate a female rancher, but he falls in love with her and switches sides.

98. THE WESTERN AIN'T DEAD YET: TWENTY-FIRST CENTURY WESTERNS

971.   Who directed and starred in *Appaloosa* in 2008?

972.   Who directed the 2007 version of *3.10 to Yuma*?

973.   Can you name the 2011 movie in which Butch Cassidy is alive and well in Bolivia?

974.   Who wrote the script for the 2005 Australian-based western *The Proposition*?

975.   Who directed and starred in *The Three Burials of Melquiades Estrada* in 2005?

976.   In *Shanghai Noon* (2000) what name does Jackie Chan call "a terrible name for a cowboy?"

977.   Which former James Bond starred in 2007's *Seraphim Falls*?

978.   Who plays Tonto in the 2013 version of the *Lone Ranger* tales?

979.   Which two real-life characters does Mattie Ross meet at the climax of 2010's *True Grit*?

980.   Who won the best supporting actor Oscar in 2013 for his performance in *Django Unchained*?

99. THE GREAT DIRECTORS HOWARD HAWKS

981. In which year was Howard Hawks born?

982. In *The Big Sky* (1952) Kirk Douglas has what body part chopped off?

983. What was Howard Hawks' last movie?

984. After watching John Wayne's performance in Hawks' *Red River*, who remarked, "I never knew the big son of a bitch could act!"

985. Hawks reportedly made 1959's *Rio Bravo* as a riposte to which classic liberal western?

986. John Carpenter's *Assault on Precinct 13* was a loose remake of which Hawks western?

987. In *El Dorado* (1966), Mississippi (James Caan) frequently quotes from a poem by which great author?

988. In 1990, which Hawks western was selected by the Library of Congress for preservation in The United States Film Registry?

989. In 1948's *Red River*, Montgomery Clift wore a hat given to him by Hawks that once belonged to which iconic western star?

990. Which Hawks movie was the last film to be shown in the cinema in Peter Bogdanovich's *The Last Picture Show*?

100. GREAT WESTERN CHARACTER ACTORS

Many a western has been enlivened by the presence of the great character actors so beloved by movie audiences. Can you name the actors who played these roles?

991. Perly Sweet in *Three Godfathers* (1948)

992. Percy Garris in *Butch Cassidy and the Sundance Kid* (1969)

993. Long Tom in *Bend of the River* (1952)

994. Judge Tolliver in *Ride the High Country* (1962)

995. Sergeant James Gregory in *The Glory Guys* (1965)

996. Ben Hindeman in *The Burning Hills* (1956)

997. Josiah Bannerman in *Stranger on Horseback* (1955)

998. Tom Grundy in *Bend of the River* (1952)

999. Morley Chase in *Decision at Sundown* (1957)

1000. Teeler Yacey in *Red River* (1948)

101. WESTERN SPEAK

The western movie occupies a world of its own with its own language. Do you know the definition of these much-loved western movie terms?

1001. Tin Horn

1002. Dry Gulch

1003. Four Flusher

1004. Carpetbagger

1005. Tenderfoot

1006. Sodbuster

1007. Corn dodger

1008. Neck-tie party.

1009. Dude

1010. Rot-gut

102. CONTEMPARY WESTERNS

1011. How many Oscars did *No Country for Old Men* (2007) win?

1012. In *The Misfits* (1961) what is the ultimate fate of the horses that are rounded up?

1013. In *Hud* (1963) how does Hud suggest that his father gets rid of the cattle that have been infected with foot and mouth disease?

1014. And can you name the author of and the novel upon which *Hud* was based?

1015. Can you name the cult director of *Lone Star* (1995)?

1016. Which 1992 movie is set on a Native American reservation in South Dakota?

1017. *Comes a Horseman* (1978) was set in which decade?

1018. Sheriff Tim Horn is a character in which classic contemporary western?

1019. In *The Electric Horseman* (1979) what does Robert Redford's washed-up rodeo-star advertise?

1020. Who wrote the original novel *All the Pretty Horses*, which was filmed in 2000?

103. WESTERN ICONS: AUDIE MURPHY

1021. In which year was Audie Murphy born?

1022. What was Audie Murphy's first western?

1023. In 1954, Murphy starred as the title character in a remake of a famous James Stewart movie. Name the Murphy movie.

1024. And in 1957, Murphy and Stewart were cast as brothers in which western?

1025. Name the 1959 western in which Murphy was cast as a hired killer.

1026. What was the name of Audie Murphy's autobiography?

1027. What is Audie Murphy's unique, non-film-related claim to fame?

1028. Name the western in which Murphy starred with a cast made up almost entirely of women.

1029. Can you name the movie in which Murphy appeared as an ageing Jesse James?

1030. In which circumstances did Audie Murphy die?

104. NAME THE YEAR

Can you recall the year that these westerns were released?

1031. *Bugles in the Afternoon*

1032. *Chisum*

1033. *Gunman's Walk*

1034. *The Horse Soldiers*

1035. *These Thousand Hills*

1036. *Silver Lode*

1037. *Santee*

1038. *Mackenna's Gold*

1039. *Maverick*

1040. *Silver River*

105. WESTERN LOCATIONS

Can you name the famous locations of these westerns?

1041. John Wayne filmed many of his latter day westerns such as *Chisum* and *The Sons of Katie Elder* in which Mexican location?

1042. *One Eyed Jacks* (1961) had an unusual setting for a western. Where was it filmed?

1043. In *Butch Cassidy and the Sundance Kid* where was the famous cliff top jump filmed?

1044. Which cult 1973 movie began and ended in Monument Valley?

1045. Classic western *Shane* was filmed in Wyoming. Can you name the mountain range that is filmed so beautifully in the movie?

1046. *The Naked Spur* (1953) was filmed entirely in which location?

1047. Nineties box office smashes *Forrest Gump* and *Back to the Future 3* were partially filmed in which iconic western location?

1048. *Cowboys and Aliens, The Missing,* and *City Slickers* were filmed in Plaza Blanca (The White Place). In which U.S. state is Plaza Blanca?

1049. What region of Spain is known as Mini-Hollywood due to the plethora of movies including many westerns filmed there?

1050. Budd Boetticher once said, "The good Lord made this place for movies." What iconic western location was Budd talking about?

106. A MAN'S (OR A WOMAN'S) GOTTA DO. . .

Countless westerns have been built around the theme of revenge. Can you identify these revenge westerns from the clues?

1051. A young man seeks vengeance on the killers who murdered his parents, even going to the extent of getting himself sent to jail in the middle of a swamp to kill one of the murderers.

1052. A cowboy's girlfriend is murdered by a gang of thieves led by a charismatic female to gain revenge.

1053. A lone avenger pursues four men who killed his wife, and discovers that he is no better than his quarry.

1054. An outlaw swears revenge on his former partner in crime, now a sheriff, who left him to take the rap for a bank robbery.

1055. A widowed woman is taught to shoot by a gunfighter so that she can kill the three men who murdered her husband.

1056. A sheriff hunts the killer of his wife and discovers that the murderer is the son of his best friend.

1057. Clay Lomax, just released from jail, is looking for the man who betrayed him, but finds his search hindered by an eight-year-old girl who may be his daughter.

1058. In this low-budget, existentialist western, a woman seeks revenge for the murders of her husband and child, and she recruits three men including a psychopathic gunslinger to help her.

1059. The Wild Bunch's William Holden and Ernest Borgnine were reunited in 1972 for this tale of a rancher seeking revenge on those who massacred his family.

1060. A former Mexican lawman is humiliated by a wealthy land baron and his henchmen. He takes the rancher's mistress captive to force the rancher into paying compensation to the widow of a man the rancher has forced him to kill.

107. LUST IN THE DUST!

1061. Name the western that was also know in tongue-in-cheek fashion as "Lust in the Dust."

1062. And can you name the actors who played the lovers in the above movie?

1063. Who directed the movie?

1064. How did the movie end?

1065. There really was a western called *Lust in the Dust!* It was made in 1985 starring which over-the-top performer?

1066. What song does Jane Russell sing when taking a bath in 1952's *Son of Paleface*?

1067. And talking of Jane Russell, what was the name of her character in *The Outlaw* (1943)?

1068. Fill in the blanks in this tagline used to promote *The Outlaw.* "What are the ___ _____ for Jane Russell's rise to stardom?"

1069. What certificate was the *The Outlaw* given by the British film censors?

1070. Who was eventually credited as the director of *The Outlaw*?

108. CLINT'S QUOTES

Can you recall the movies that these great Clint quotes come from?

1071. "Wonder what took her so long to get mad?"

1072. "Get three coffins ready. . . ."

1073. "It's a hell of a thing killin' a man. You take away all he's got and all he's ever gonna have."

1074. "Dyin' ain't much of a living, boy."

1075. "Sister, I don't mind shootin' 'em for ya, but I'll be damned if I'm gonna sweat over 'em for ya."

1076. "You see, in this world there's two kinds of people, my friend: Those with loaded guns and those who dig. You dig."

1077. "I know it's a crappy deal buddy."

1078. "I'm going after them and I'm going alone. Our partnership is dissolved."

1079. "But I've always been lucky when it comes to killing folks."

1080. "Are you gonna pull those pistols or whistle Dixie?"

109. WESTERN ICONS: GLENN FORD

1081. In which year was Glenn Ford born?

1082. Which famous actress and dancer was Ford's first wife?

1083. Who played Ford's love interest in *The Sheepman* (1958)?

1084. Ford starred in *Jubal* in 1956, which is considered a western remake of which Shakespearian tragedy?

1085. Can you name Ford's 1949 western that was partly shot in Arizona's Superstition Mountains?

1086. *The Americano* (1955) starring Ford, was set in which country?

1087. Can you recall the name of Ford's 1971 television series set in Madrid County?

1088. Ford played the character Ben Wade in which classic western?

1089. Can you name the budding superstar who received his first screen credit in Ford's 1967 western *A Time for Dying*?

1090. Ford starred in 1951's *The Redhead and the Cowboy*. Who played the redhead?

110. CLASSIC WESTERN SCENES

1091. A stagecoach is brought to a halt by a single off screen gun shot. The camera cuts to a lone cowboy with a saddle in one hand and a rifle in the other. The cowboy twirls the rifle and shouts "Hold it!" The camera zooms in on a close up of the cowboy's face, and briefly loses focus. It is one of the great star entrances in movie history. Name the star and the movie.

1092. A horse soldier escorting two settlers is ambushed by Apaches. The soldier shoots the female settler and makes a run for it with the woman's son. His horse is felled, and the soldier shoots himself to avoid a lingering and agonising death at the hands of the Apaches. Name the movie.

1093. In a memorable scene of this ground-breaking film, a gunman points his revolver directly at the camera and the audience and fires the gun six times from point-blank range. Name the film and, for an extra point, the actor.

1094. In the opening scene of this classic western, a penniless drunk is desperate for a whisky in a cantina and attempts to fish a dollar out of a spittoon, but is stopped by a boot kicking the spittoon away. The drunk reacts by clubbing the owner of the boot over the head with a stick. Name the movie.

1095. The camera focuses on the hero's agony as he is grabbed by the villain's henchmen and shot through the hand. Name the actor who is shot and the movie.

1096. Two men slug it out in a violent fight in the middle of a vast twilight lit prairie. Much of the fight is filmed in long shot, and only ends when one of the men gasps, "I've just about had enough, if it's alright with you." Name the actors and the movie.

1097. Two women, one dressed in black the other in a bright yellow shirt and red scarf, have a gun fight to the death on a mountain-top cabin veranda. Name the movie.

1098. In one of the most memorable tracking shots in cinema, Randolph Scott rides   down from the hills shooting at some "dry gulchin'" Southern trash. His horse is shot out from under him, but he recovers to fight on. What is the movie?

1099. Two former friends, now adversaries, meet up again at either side of a bridge. One takes aim with a rifle at the other who doffs his hat just as the bridge blows up. Name the movie.

1100. In a restaurant, a memorable screen villain tries to intimidate a one-armed stranger but gets his just deserts when the stranger gives him a lesson in karate. Name the movie and the villain.

111 BEHIND THE SCENES

The western genre would be much poorer without the contributions of many unsung professionals behind the scenes.

1101. Can you name the legendary stunt man who worked in hundreds of westerns and doubled for John Wayne in *Stagecoach*?

1102. Can you name the scriptwriter of six John Ford westerns including *The Searchers*?

1103. Conrad Hall won a best cinematography Oscar. For which movie?

1104. Richard Hageman won an Oscar for his music for which 1939 western?

1105. Who sang the theme song to *High Noon*?

1106. Can you name the twenty-five-year-old composer of the soundtrack to *Bad Day at Black Rock*?

1107. Who was the distinguished cinematographer whose photography illuminated classic westerns such as *Ride the High Country, True Grit,* and *The Wild Bunch*?

1108. Who produced the 1939 version of *Stagecoach*?

1109. Who composed the score for *The Searchers*?

1110. Can you name the stuntman and actor who frequently doubled for John Wayne and appeared in several of his movies such as *McLintock!* and *The War Wagon*?

112 WESTERN ICONS: RICHARD WIDMARK

1111. In which year was Richard Widmark born?

1112. Can you name the John Sturges western in which Widmark played Jim Slater, a survivor of the Gila Valley massacre in Arizona?

1113. Which famous actor played Widmark's father and the tyrannical patriarch of his family in 1954's *Broken Lance*?

1114. Richard Widmark played a character in a western with the same name as a character from *Rio Bravo*. What was the western and what was the character's name?

1115. In *The Law and Jake Wade* (1958) what does Widmark's character say to Jake Wade when Wade throw's Widmark's gun away?

1116. There is an airport named after Richard Widmark—true or false?

1117. What do these Richard Widmark westerns all have in common? *Yellow Sky, Garden of Evil, Broken Lance, The Law and Jake Wade, The Alamo, Death of a Gunfighter.*

1118. How many westerns did Widmark make with John Ford?

1119. In *Warlock* (1959), what injury is inflicted on Widmark's character by the leader of the cowboy gang?

1120. In which year did Richard Widmark die?

113. DUKE'S QUOTES

Name the movie these great John Wayne quotes come from.

1121. "Put an Amen to it."

1122. "Fill your hands, you son of a bitch!"

1123. "Somebody ought to punch you on the nose. But I won't, I won't. The hell I will!"

1124. "Sorry don't get it done, Dude."

1125. "I'm looking at a tin star with a drunk pinned to it."

1126. "Well, there are some things a man just can't run away from."

1127. "I won't be wronged, I won't be insulted, and I won't be laid a hand on. I don't do these things to other people, and I require the same from them."

1128. "Mine was taller!"

1129. "Let's go home, Debbie."

1130. "You may need me and this Winchester, Curly."

114. REVISIONIST WESTERNS

1131. "I came a thousand miles to kill you," is a line from which Anthony Mann western?

1132. Can you name the blacklisted director of 1969's *Tell Them Willie Boy Is Here*?

1133. Who played Wild Bill Hickok in Walter Hill's *Wild Bill* (1995)?

1134. In *McCabe and Mrs Miller* (1971) how does McCabe die, and what song plays over his death scene?

1135. Wyoming's bid for statehood forms the background for which 1999 television western?

1136. In *The Missing* (2003) what is the English translation of Tommy Lee Jones's character's name Chaa-duu-ba-itsidan?

1137. Boss Spearman is a character in which 2003 revisionist western?

1138. Director Monte Hellman shot two back-to-back revisionist westerns in 1965 in the Utah desert in just thirty-five days. Can you name them?

1139. "This time we do it right," is a famous line from which legendary western?

1140. 1977's *The White Buffalo* starred Charles Bronson as which legendary western figure?

115. EXPERT WESTERN STALWARTS

1141. Michael Pate was a versatile Australian actor who appeared in many westerns. What was unusual about his role in 1959's *Curse of the Undead*?

1142. I was born in 1926 and was the object of the creature's desire in *The Creature from the Black Lagoon*. I appeared in twenty westerns. I changed my name from Betty to Julia, but I am better known as. . . . ?

1143. Which western stalwart plays the train driver who pleads with James Stewart not to burn his train in *Shenandoah*?

1144. This western stalwart was the father-in-law of Harry Carey Junior, and John Wayne reputedly copied his walk.

1145. I was resident bad guy in many westerns of the 1940s and 1950s, such as *Vera Cruz* and *Bend of the River*, but I came off second best to the snow and Robert Ryan in *Day of the Outlaw* in 1959.

1146. This western stalwart played Jesse James twice and also Billy the Kid, but he is better known for his Red Ryder serial.

1147. Who played Monte Walsh's friend Chet, in 1970's *Monte Walsh*?

1148. I was born in 1925 and I could play good guys and bad guys. In fact that was the name of one of my westerns. Who am I?

1149. Allan Lane made numerous low-budget oaters in the 1940s and 1950s. What was his nickname, and what was the name of his horse?

1150. I helped Bogie shelter from the rain in a famous film noir. I then appeared in seventeen oaters, before moving from horse operas to a famous television soap opera. Who am I?

116. EXPERT CLINT

1151. Name the Clint movie in which the title credits disappear as if being shot with a gun.

1152. In which movie does the ill treatment of Clint's mule provoke a gun fight?

1153. Who did Clint replace as director of *The Outlaw Josey Wales* (1976)?

1154. Can you name the pair of pistols Clint uses to great effect in *The Outlaw Josey Wales*?

1155. What book is Megan reading when The Preacher first rides into view in *Pale Rider* (1985)?

1156. Clint starred in *Joe Kidd* in 1972. Can you recall the movie's spectacular climax?

1157. Which Eastwood western was criticised thus...? "If only the actors hadn't got in the way of all this beautiful scenery, it would have been a great film."

1158. In *Coogan's Bluff* (1968) what state does Coogan hail from?

1159. Who links Eastwood's 1985 western *Pale Rider* with rock legend Neil Young?

1160. "Don't piss down my back and tell me it's raining." Can you name the actor in *The Outlaw Josey Wales* who spoke those oft-quoted words?

117. EXPERT WESTERN QUOTES

Name the westerns that these great quotes come from, and the actors who said them.

1161. "You're a good-looking boy. You've big, broad shoulders. But he's a man. And it takes more than big, broad shoulders to make a man."

1162. "Get ready, little lady. Hell is coming to breakfast."

1163. "The only real Americans in this merry old parish are on the other side of that ridge with feathers in their hair."

1164. "Ain't no rules in a knife fight!"

1165. "We lost. We always lose."

1166. "Here I am, thirty five years old and I ain't even got a good watch."

1167. "That's a lot of man you're carrying in those boots, stranger."

1168. "When I was a boy, men didn't live long enough to become grampas."

1169. "We'll fool St. Peter yet."

1170. "I must have killed more men than Cecil B. DeMille."

118. EXPERT WESTERN ICONS

1171. Can you name the three western movie legends that Larry McMurtry originally intended to cast for a movie version of his book *Lonesome Dove*?

1172. John Wayne's son Patrick played his son in *Big Jake* in 1971. Which other western icon's son also starred as The Duke's son in the movie?

1173. What type of horse did Randolph Scott ride in many of his later westerns?

1174. In *The War Wagon* (1967) what is Kirk Douglas wearing when he answers the door to John Wayne? And what does Wayne call him?

1175. Which western icon recently revealed that earlier in his career he turned down the roles of James Bond and Superman?

1176. In *Forty Guns* (1957) Jessica Drummond (Barbara Stanwyck) tells Griff Bonell (Barry Sullivan) that she had been bitten by a rattlesnake when she was fifteen. What was his reply?

1177. Can you name the western icon who claimed that he had only two styles of acting: "with or without a hat?"

1178. Can you name the western icon and the Australian western in which he appeared in a dual role in 1982?

1179. Which two western icons played the same role seventeen years apart in versions of a Zane Grey novel?

1180. What was Randolph Scott's character's name in *Comanche Station* (1960) and what was his mission?

119. EXPERT JOHN WAYNE

1181. Who presented John Wayne with his Oscar for *True Grit*?

1182. In the climax of *The Searchers*, Wayne holds his right arm with his left hand in a tribute to which actor?

1183. What memento from *Red River* did Duke wear in many of his subsequent westerns?

1184. Can you name the movie in which John Wayne refers to James Stewart as Pilgrim?

1185. John Wayne was born Marion Michael Morrison. True or false?

1186. Can you name the movie in which Duke's character was smacked over the head with a shovel by a character named Paul Regret?

1187. How was Wayne billed when he guest starred in an episode of *Wagon Train*?

1188. Who was responsible for this quote? "People identify with me, but dream of being John Wayne."

1189. In which movie did Maureen O'Hara describe Wayne's character as "an extremely harsh, unpleasant kind of man?"

1190. What was John Wayne's last ever movie line?

120. EXPERT WESTERN TRIVIA

1191.   What was the first western to be given an X-rating?

1192.   Howard Hawks's sci-fi horror *The Thing* (1952) featured a young actor as the Thing, who would subsequently become one of the most loved western television actors. Who was he?

1193.   The actress who played Constance Towers's maid in *The Horse Soldiers* (1959) had a sporting claim to fame. What was it?

1194.   What western movie has the longest introductory title sequence in film history?

1195.   How many versions of *The Squaw Man* did legendary director Cecil B. DeMille make?

1196.   *City of Bad Men* (1953) had which famous boxing match as its backdrop?

1197.   Can you name the four sets of actor brothers in 1980's *The Long Riders*?

1198.   What town does the 3.10 to Yuma leave from?

1199.   Can you name the 1980 science-fiction film that was a pastiche of *The Magnificent Seven*?

1200.   And following on from the previous question, who reprised their role from *The Magnificent Seven* in the movie?

121. EXPERT CLASSIC WESTERNS

1201. Which classic western was called "Grand Hotel on Wheels," by *New Yorker* magazine?

1202. Can you name all six actors who have possession of the fabled rifle in the 1950 version of *Winchester '73*?

1203. What are Little Bill Daggett's last words in *Unforgiven* (1992)?

1204. In *Rio Bravo* (1959), how does Dude (Dean Martin) discover the murderer, who he pursued into Burdette's saloon, is hiding in the loft of the saloon?

1205. Can you name the classic western in which the Cheyenne call themselves "The Human Beings?"

1206. In the two cinematic versions of *True Grit*, there is one fundamental difference in the appearance of the two actors who play Rooster Coburn. What is it?

1207. The writer of *High Noon* was later black listed from Hollywood. Can you name him?

1208. In *The Magnificent Seven*, what is Britt's reply when Chico tells him that Britt has just made the greatest shot he has ever seen?

1209. The title of which classic western does not appear until the end of the final scene?

1210. Can you name the actors who played the five Hammond brothers in 1962's *Ride the High Country*?

122. EXPERT
TELEVISION WESTERNS

1211. Ennio Morricone wrote the theme tune to which 1970 western series?

1212. Name the actor who played both Daniel Boone and Davy Crockett on television.

1213. By what name was William Anderson Hatfield (Kevin Costner) known in the 2012 television miniseries *Hatfields and McCoys*?

1214. Who played *The Lazarus Man* on television in 1996, and whose bodyguard was he?

1215. What was the name of the 1970s television series about two brothers searching for their sister who had been kidnapped by Indians?

1216. What was the name of the short-lived 1970s western series starring James Garner as a reluctant sheriff in small town Arizona?

1217. How is Orison Whipple Hungerford Jr. better known?

1218. Who directed the 2006 western miniseries *Broken Trail*?

1219. Who was the English actor who played the owner of the Shiloh Ranch in *The Men from Shiloh*?

1220. Who played trail boss Gil Favor in *Rawhide*?

123. HOW THE WEST WAS WON

1221. What was the subject of Fritz Lang's *Western Union* (1941)?

1222. In *The Far Horizons* (1955), who played the famous explorers Meriwether Lewis and William Clark?

1223. Steven Spielberg produced a western television series in 2005, documenting the lives of a settler family and a Native American family in the west. What was it called?

1224. Who narrated the 1962 western *How the West Was Won*?

1225. Who played the title role in *Kit Carson* in 1940?

1226. Which famous director directed 1939's *Union Pacific*, a movie that told the story of the building of the railroad across the American West?

1227. Can you name the 1967 western that told the story of a wagon train settlers travelling between Missouri and Oregon in the 1840s?

1228. *The Pony Express* (1953) told the story of how the mail route from Missouri to California was established, and it featured two real-life western figures. Who were they, and can you name the actors who played them?

1229. The television series *Hell on Wheels* revolved around which event in American history?

1230. *The Last Command* (1955) told the story of events at which famous battle?

124. THE LAST ROUND UP

1231. Can you name the 1971 western starring Charles Bronson that featured samurai warriors?

1232. "Who are those guys?" is a famous line from one of the greatest ever westerns. Name the film and the actor who spoke the line.

1233. Can you name the four actresses who played the *Bad Girls* in 1994?

1234. Can you name the three sequels to *The Magnificent Seven*?

1235. Which 1980s box office smash was described by its director as a western without cowboys?

1236. What was Jack Lemmon's only western movie?

1237. The western novel *Riders of the Purple Sage* has been filmed many times. Who was the author of the book?

1238. In the *Star Trek* Episode "Spectre of the Gun," Captain Kirk and his crew find themselves embroiled in which famous wild west incident?

1239. And which actor from Star Trek featured in the 1971 western *Catlow*?

1240. Quentin Tarantino won an Oscar for *Django Unchained* in 2013. In which category?

125. CLOSING LINES

Can you identify the westerns from these closing lines?

1241. "Hey Blond!! You know what you are? Just a dirty son-of-a-b...!"

1242. "He was called John Russell."

1243. "I'll see you later."

1244. "Little bob-cat"

1245. "You've earned it"

1246. "Good. For a moment there, I thought we were in trouble."

1247. "Well, come see a fat old man sometime!"

1248. "I reckon so. I guess we all died a little in that damn war."

1249. "You better not cut up nor otherwise harm no whores, or I'll come back and kill every one of you sons of bitches."

1250. "That was Ace's mistake."

ANSWERS

1. OPENING LINES
1 *Shane* (1953)
2 *Only the Valiant* (1951)
3 *No Country for Old Men* (2007)
4 *The Assassination of Jesse James by the Coward Bob Ford* (2007)
5 *Jeremiah Johnson* (1972)
6 *Shenandoah* (1965)
7 *The Wild Bunch* (1969)
8 *Rio Bravo* (1959)
9 *The Ballad of Cable Hogue* (1970)
10 *Little Big Man* (1970)

2. JESSE JAMES
11 Tyrone Power
12 Robert Wagner
13 Robert Duvall
14 Lawrence Tierney
15 Brad Pitt
16 Wendell Corey
17 Colin Farrell
18 Reed Hadley
19 John Lupton
20 Rob Lowe

3. TITLE ROLES
21 Robert Redford
22 Charlton Heston

23 Glenn Ford
24 Gene Tierney
25 William Holden
26 Barbara Stanwyck
27 Clint Walker
28 Audie Murphy
29 Robert Walker Jr.
30 Sterling Hayden

4. NAME THE DIRECTOR
31 William Wellman
32 George Stevens
33 Fred Zinnemann
34 Delmer Daves
35 Henry King
36 William Wyler
37 Ralph Nelson
38 Martin Ritt
39 Robert Aldrich
40 Walter Hill

5. LEADING LADIES
41 Lillian Gish
42 Olivia de Havilland
43 Teresa Wright
44 Joan Collins
45 Shelley Winters
46 Elsa Martinelli
47 Angie Dickinson
48 Joan Hackett
49 Katherine Ross
50 Annette Bening

6. WESTERN TRIVIA 1
51 John Wayne, Dean Martin, Earl Holliman, and
   Michael Anderson
52 Rueben
53 *The Carpetbaggers* by Harold Robbins

54 Lillie Langtry
55 Sophia Loren
56 *Love Me Tender* (1956)
57 Rodeo Riders
58 Warren Zevon
59 *Santa Fe Trail* (1940)
60 Leslie Nielsen

7. WESTERN QUOTES
61 Gregory Peck in *The Gunfighter* (1950)
62 Pernell Roberts in *Ride Lonesome* (1959)
63 Bob Hope in *The Paleface* (1948)
64 William Holden in *The Wild Bunch* (1969)
65 Gary Cooper in *The Virginian* (1929) and Joel McCrea in *The Virginian* (1946)
66 John Wayne in *True Grit* (1969)
67 Joel McCrea in *Ride the High Country* (1962)
68 Steve McQueen in *The Magnificent Seven* (1960)
69 Cleavon Little in *Blazing Saddles* (1974)
70 Paul Newman in *Butch Cassidy and the Sundance Kid* (1969)

8. WYATT EARP
71 Randolph Scott
72 Henry Fonda
73 Will Geer
74 James Millican
75 Ronald Reagan
76 Burt Lancaster
77 Hugh O'Brian
78 James Garner
79 Harris Yulin
80 Kevin Costner

9. REAL NAMES
81 Ray Milland   Reginald Truscott Jones
82 Robert Taylor   Spangler Arlington Brugh
83 Kirk Douglas   Issur Danielovitch
84 Jack Palance   Volodymyr Palahniuk

85 Charlton Heston   Charles Carter
86 Jeff Chandler   Ira Grossel
87 Slim Pickens   Louis Burton Lindley Junior
88 Gene Wilder   Jerome Silberman
89 Roy Rogers   Leonard Slye
90 Rock Hudson   Roy Scherer Junior

10. WESTERN TRIVIA 2

91 Jeffrey Hunter
92 *Dodge City* (1939)
93 *Bad Company*
94 Bruce Willis
95 Max Sand
96 Yul Brynner
97 Trigger
98 Charles Bronson
99 A retired sea captain.
100 Jay Silverheels who played Tonto in *The Lone Ranger.*

11. WESTERN OSCARS

101 Warner Baxter (best actor)
102 Gary Cooper (best actor)
103 John Wayne (best actor)
104 Gene Hackman (best supporting actor)
105 Anthony Quinn (best supporting actor)
106 Thomas Mitchell (best supporting actor)
107 Walter Brennan (best supporting actor)
108 Jack Palance (best supporting actor)
109 Burl Ives (best supporting actor)
110 Lee Marvin (best actor)

12. SOUNDTRACKS

111 Jerome Moross
112 Elmer Bernstein
113 Ennio Morricone
114 John Barry
115 Ry Cooder
116 Bob Dylan

117 Dimitri Tiomkin
118 John Williams
119 Burt Bacharach
120 Bruce Broughton

13. BAD GUYS
121 Richard Boone in *Hombre* (1967)
122 Ian MacDonald in *High Noon* (1952)
123 Karl Malden in *One Eyed Jacks* (1961)
124 Jack Palance in *Shane* (1953)
125 Stephen McNally in *Winchester '73* (1950)
126 Henry Brandon in *The Searchers* (1956)
127 George Kennedy in *Lonely Are the Brave* (1962)
128 Gene Hackman in *Unforgiven* (1992)
129 Richard Widmark in *The Law and Jake Wade* (1958)
130 Lee Marvin in *The Comancheros* (1961)

14. GOOD GUYS
131 Joseph Cotton
132 Yul Brynner
133 Rock Hudson
134 Van Heflin
135 James Garner
136 Stewart Granger
137 William Holden
138 Harry Carey
139 Audie Murphy
140 Henry Fonda

15. TELEVISION WESTERNS 1
141 *Bonanza*
142 *Alias Smith and Jones*
143 *Deadwood*
144 *Tales of Wells Fargo*
145 *The Virginian*
146 *Lonesome Dove*
147 *Have Gun Will Travel*
148 *The High Chaparral*

149 *Gunsmoke*
150 *Wagon Train*

16. THE FILM OF THE BOOK

151 Glendon Swarthout
152 Charles Portis
153 Thomas Eidson (book title *The Last Ride*)
154 Alan LeMay
155 Walter van Tilburg Clark
156 Jack Schaefer
157 Elmore Leonard
158 Owen Wister
159 Thomas Berger
160 Louis L'Amour

17. WESTERN WOMEN

161 Barbara Stanwyck
162 Raquel Welch
163 Michele Carey
164 Kim Darby
165 Sharon Stone
166 Shelley Winters
167 Joanne Dru
168 Doris Day
169 Mercedes McCambridge
170 Judith Anderson

18. NATIVE AMERICANS 1

171 Kiowa
172 Comanche
173 Apache
174 Sioux
175 Cheyenne
176 Seminole
177 Nez Perce
178 Navajo
179 Shoshone
180 Blackfoot

19. COMEDY WESTERNS
181 Bob Hope in *The Paleface* (1948)
182 The Marx Brothers
183 *Son of Paleface* (1952)
184 *The Taming of the Shrew*
185 Jason McCullough in *Support Your Local Sheriff* (1969)
186 Trigger
187 Johnson
188 Brushwood Gulch
189 He stirs his cigar in Jumbo's coffee and then stubs it out in his lunch.
190 John Astin

20. TELEVISION WESTERNS 2
191 The Ponderosa
192 Joshua (Smith) and Thaddeus (Jones)
193 Kid Curry was Jones and Hannibal Hayes was Smith.
194 James Arness
195 *The Monroes*
196 Eric, played by Dan Blocker.
197 Medicine Bow
198 Scout
199 Clayton Moore
200 David Carradine

21. DUKE'S LADIES
201 Marguerite Churchill
202 Ella Raines
203 Gail Russell
204 Vera Ralston
205 Maureen O'Hara
206 Geraldine Page
207 Angie Dickinson
208 Capucine
209 Katherine Hepburn
210 Lauren Bacall

22. WESTERN ICONS: RANDOLPH SCOTT
211 North Carolina (in 1898)
212 True
213 *Ride Lonesome* (1959)
214 Seven
215 Agry
216 The Battle of the Little Big Horn.
217 The Statler Brothers
218 *Ride the High Country* (1962)
219 *Shoot-Out at Medicine Bend* (1957)
220 1987

23. MORE BAD GUYS
221 Harvey Korman in *Blazing Saddles* (1974)
222 Kris Kristofferson in *Lone Star* (1995)
223 Eli Wallach in *The Magnificent Seven* (1960)
224 Arthur Kennedy in *The Man from Laramie* (1955)
225 Eric Schweig in *The Missing* (2003)
226 Emile Meyer in *Shane* (1953)
227 Zachary Scott in *Colt 45* (1950)
228 Dan Duryea in *Winchester '73* (1950)
229 Michael Gambon in *Open Range* (2003)
230 Javier Bardem in *No Country for Old Men* (2007)

24. WESTERN SIDEKICKS
231 Walter Brennan
232 Millard Mitchell
233 Henry Morgan
234 Oliver Hardy
235 Arthur Hunnicutt
236 George "Gabby" Hayes
237 Jack Elam
238 Chill Wills
239 Alan Hale
240 Andy Clyde

25. WHO ARE THOSE GUYS?
241 William Holden in *The Wild Bunch* (1969)

242 Jeffrey Hunter in *The Searchers* (1956)
243 Martin Balsam in *Hombre* (1967)
244 Joel McCrea in *Ride the High Country* (1962)
245 Henry Fonda in *Fort Apache* (1948)
246 Robert Mitchum in *The Wonderful Country* (1959)
247 James Stewart in *Bend of the River* (1952)
248 Clark Gable in *The Misfits* (1961)
249 Gary Cooper in *Vera Cruz* (1954)
250 James Coburn in *A Fistful of Dynamite* (1971)

26. MORE WESTERN QUOTES
251 *Open Range* (2003)
252 *Tombstone* (1993)
253 *Red River* (1948)
254 *Butch Cassidy and the Sundance Kid* (1969)
255 *City Slickers* (1991)
256 *Monte Walsh* (1970 and 2003)
257 *Shane* (1953)
258 *The Magnificent Seven* (1960)
259 *Once Upon a Time in the West* (1968)
260 *Blazing Saddles* (1974)

27. DUKE'S ROLES
261 *Red River* (1948)
262 *She Wore a Yellow Ribbon* (1949)
263 *Rio Grande* (1950)
264 *The Comancheros* (1961)
265 *Rio Lobo* (1970)
266 *El Dorado* (1966)
267 *Three Godfathers* (1948)
268 *The War Wagon* (1967)
269 *Angel and the Badman* (1947)
270 *Dark Command* (1940)

28. WESTERN TRIVIA 3
271 *The Missouri Breaks* (1976)
272 *The Adams Family* – Ted Cassidy played Lurch.
273 *My Darling Clementine* (1946)

274 *Dodge City* (1939). The band Pure Prairie League were named after a temperance union in the movie.

275 Whiskey

276 William Conrad (he played Frank Cannon)

277 *Blazing Saddles* (1974) played by Mel Brooks.

278 Roger Corman

279 Stetson City

280 *The Godfather* (1972)

29. LAWMEN

281 Richard Widmark in *Death of a Gunfighter* (1969)

282 William Conrad in *The Ride Back* (1957)

283 John Wayne in *Rio Bravo* (1959)

284 Brian Dennehy in *Silverado* (1985)

285 Chris Cooper in *Lone Star* (1995)

286 Robert Mitchum in *El Dorado* (1966)

287 John Cleese in *Silverado* (1985)

288 Burt Lancaster in *Lawman* (1970)

289 Henry Fonda in *Warlock* (1959)

290 Kirk Douglas in *Last Train from Gun Hill* (1959)

30. CLASSIC WESTERNS

291 Claire Trevor

292 Bolivia

293 *High Noon*

294 He attracted attention to himself in scenes in several ways: shaking his shotgun cartridges before loading, flapping his hat, and screening the sun with his hat.

295 They both used knives, instead of guns, in duels.

296 *The Searchers*

297 Lloyd Bridges

298 One (Hatfield, played by John Carradine).

299 Stonewall

300 Four: Best Picture, Best Director, Best Supporting Actor, Best Film Editing.

31. WESTERN ICONS: GARY COOPER

301 Montana

302 True (from 1910 to 1913)
303 *The Virginian*
304 *Sergeant York* (1941)
305 John Wayne
306 *Friendly Persuasion* (1956)
307 *Alias Jesse James* (1959)
308 Melody
309 *The Plainsman* (1936)
310 1961

32. THE SILENTS
311 *The Great Train Robbery*
312 D.W. Griffith
313 Al Jennings
314 Harry Carey
315 Thomas Ince (Ince reputedly died on board William Randolph Hearst's boat).
316 *The General* (1926)
317 *The Great K and A Robbery* (1925)
318 The locomotive train.
319 Oklahoma
320 The circling of the wagons to fend off an Indian attack.

33. ALTERNATE TITLES
321 *From Hell to Texas*   *Manhunt*
322 *Ride the High Country*   *Guns in the Afternoon*
323 *The Appaloosa*   *Southwest to Sonora*
324 *Along the Great Divide* *The Travellers*
325 *Bend of the River*   *Where the River Bends*
326 *Welcome to Hard Times* *Killer on a Horse*
327 *Cheyenne*   *The Wyoming Kid*
328 *Hearts of the West*   *Hollywood Cowboy*
329 *The Violent Men*   *Rough Company*
330 *Man with the Gun*   *The Troubleshooter*

34. SONGS
331 *High Noon* (1952)
332 *The Alamo* (1960)

333 *Young Guns II* (1990)
334 *Butch Cassidy and the Sundance Kid* (1969)
335 *Calamity Jane* (1953)
336 *The Paleface* (1948) and reprised in *Son of Paleface* (1952).
337 *Oklahoma!* (1955)
338 *Son of Paleface* (1952)
339 *Will Penny* (1967)
340 *Rio Bravo* (1959)

35. STATES
341 Texas
342 Kansas
343 Wyoming
344 Nevada
345 Texas
346 South Dakota
347 California
348 Arizona
349 New Mexico
350 Kansas

36. HORSES
351 Hoot Gibson
352 Tom Mix
353 Hopalong Cassidy (William Boyd)
354 John Wayne
355 William S Hart
356 Gene Autry
357 Lash LaRue
358 James Stewart
359 Randolph Scott
360 Dale Evans

37. THE 1930s
361 James Cagney
362 Humphrey Bogart
363 The American Revolutionary War
364 *Law and Order*

365 Jean Arthur
366 Wyatt Earp
367 Michael Curtiz
368 Charles Bickford
369 His pants
370 *Cimarron*

38. WESTERN ICONS: JAMES STEWART

371 *Destry Rides Again* (1939)
372 *Dodge City*
373 Cochise
374 An English Herefordshire Bull.
375 A lawyer
376 Wyatt Earp
377 Dean Martin
378 The United States Air – Force.
379 The Accordion.
380 1997

39. TOWNS

381 *High Noon* (1952)
382 *Son of Paleface* (1952)
383 *Unforgiven* (1992)
384 *The Gunfighter* (1950)
385 *The Man who shot Liberty Valance* (1962)
386 *Kid Blue* (1973)
387 *High Plains Drifter* (1973)
388 *Blazing Saddles* (1974)
389 *Support Your Local Gunfighter* (1971)
390 *Carry on Cowboy* (1965)

40. COWBOYS

391 Lee Marvin
392 Glenn Ford
393 Joel McCrea
394 Brian Donlevy
395 Burt Lancaster
396 James Garner

397 Cliff Robertson
398 Steve McQueen
399 Montgomery Clift
400 Tom Selleck

41. NAME THE MOVIE (PHOTO)
401 *Winchester '73* (1950)
402 *Angel and the Badman* (1947)
403 *Vera Cruz* (1954)
404 *The Westerner* (1940)
405 *The Oxbow Incident* (1943)
406 *Jesse James* (1939)
407 *Hondo* (1953)
408 *Santa Fe Trail* (1940)
409 *Backlash* (1956)
410 *The Deadly Companions* (1961)

42. THE OLDEST PROFESSION
411 Claire Trevor
412 Mari Blanchard
413 Linda Darnell
414 Jo Ann Van Fleet
415 Stella Stevens
416 Julie Christie
417 Madeline Kahn
418 Shirley MacLaine
419 Jeanne Moreau
420 Cloris Leachman

43. THE GREAT WESTERN DIRECTORS: JOHN STURGES
421 *The Walking Hills* (1949)
422 John J. Macreedy
423 Nine p.m.
424 Three (Chris, Vin and Chico)
425 Robert Taylor
426 The Gunfight at the OK Coral
427 John Forsythe
428 *Joe Kidd* (1972)

429 Burt Lancaster (Earp) and Kirk Douglas (Holliday)
430 Steve McQueen, Charles Bronson and James Coburn

44. THE 1940S
431 Errol Flynn
432 Onions
433 John Wayne, Harry Carey Junior, Pedro Armendariz
434 *The Sea of Grass*
435 Alan Ladd
436 "Stretch"
437 Humphrey Bogart
438 *Canyon Passage*
439 Shirley Temple
440 Billy the Kid

45. WESTERN ICONS: JOEL MCCREA
441 1905 in California.
442 William F. Cody (Buffalo Bill)
443 There wasn't a gun fired in the entire film.
444 Frances Dee
445 They all wear bells on their spurs.
446 The two actors were originally cast to play each other's role.
447 Maureen Stapleton
448 L.Q. Jones
449 Sam Houston
450 *Mustang Country* (1976)

46. GUNFIGHTERS
451 Jack Palance in *The Lonely Man* (1957)
452 Robert Mitchum in *Man with the Gun* (1955)
453 Chuck Connors in *Support Your Local Gunfighter* (1971)
454 Glenn Ford in *The Fastest Gun Alive* (1956)
455 Stacy Keach in *The Life and Times of Judge Roy Bean* (1972)
456 Christopher George in *El Dorado* (1966)
457 John Wayne in *The Shootist* (1976)
458 Christopher Walken in *Heaven's Gate* (1981)
459 Yul Brynner in *Invitation to a Gunfighter* (1964)
460 William S. Hart in *The Gunfighter* (1917)

47. SOLDIERS
461 Spencer Tracey

462 Sydney Greenstreet

463 Gene Hackman

464 Tom Berenger

465 Martin Sheen

466 Errol Flynn

467 J. Carroll Nash

468 Harry Morgan

469 John Wayne

470 Robert Shaw

48. EARLY WESTERN STARS
471 William S Hart

472 A town

473 Harry Carey

474 Buster Keaton

475 Tom Mix

476 Hoot Gibson

477 Francis Ford

478 Richard Dix

479 Gilbert M. "Broncho Billy" Anderson

480. Buck Jones

49. GREAT BAD GUYS
481 He fired his gun at the feet of a baby girl, terrifying her.

482 John Russell

483 Tom Doniphan played by John Wayne.

484 John Carradine

485 Robert Wilke, Sheb Wooley, and Lee Van Cleef

486 One of the western's greatest bad guys: L.Q. Jones.

487 A fly

488 Hec Ramsey

489 Robert Wilke

490 Eli Wallach

50. SPAGHETTI WESTERNS 1
491 *Once Upon a Time in the West* (1968)

492 *A Fistful of Dollars* (1964)
493 *For a Few Dollars More* (1965)
494 *The Good, the Bad, and the Ugly* (1966)
495 *The Grand Silence* (1966)
496 *My Name is Trinity* (1970)
497 *My Name is Nobody* (1973)
498 *Death Rides a Horse* (1968)
499 *Face to Face* (1967)
500 *A Pistol for Ringo* (1965)

51. THE BLUE AND THE GREY
501 John Jakes
502 A Union soldier is about to bayonet the boy but stops. It is the boy's friend Gabriel, a freed slave who has joined the Union Army. Gabriel hides the boy and then rejoins the battle.
503 James Coburn
504 Ang Lee
505 Starlings
506 *Journey to Shiloh*
507 John Ford
508 *The Raid* (1951)
509 *Run of the Arrow* (1957)
510 A hotel

52. RACISM
511 Woody Strode
512 He shoots out the corpse's eyes in the belief that a Comanche without eyes will be unable to enter the spirit world after death.
513 Audie Murphy
514 *Flaming Star* (1960)
515 They ask the stagecoach driver to tell him that he is not welcome inside the stage and must ride up top.
516 They take over a hearse and ride it to boot hill to enable a corpse to be buried. The townspeople had refused to allow the burial as the dead man was an Indian.
517 A Japanese farmer had been murdered by the townspeople after the bombing of Pearl Harbour.

518 He frames him on a false rustling charge, and the boy is later lynched.
519 Chato kills a racist lawman in self-defence.
520 *The Last Hunt* (1956)

53. SHOOT-OUTS
521 Aces and eights
522 Will played by Gary Grimes
523 Johnny Cash
524 Richard Boone, Hugh O'Brien, Bill McKinney
525 Anthony Quinn
526 He removes the badge from his shirt and throws it to the ground.
527 "I've heard that you're a low down Yankee liar."
528 Lancaster grins, twirls his gun and puts it back in its holster. He then topples to the ground, dying.
529 *The Woman They Almost Lynched* (1953)
530 The Mexican General slits Angel's throat.

54. WESTERN ICONS: BARBARA STANWYCK
531 *The Great Man's Lady* (1944)
532 *The Big Valley*
533 Ruby Stevens
534 A ranch
535 *Cattle Queen of Montana* (1956)
536 *Forty Guns* (1957)
537 *The Maverick Queen* (1956)
538 "She's a high-riding woman with a whip."
539 *Trooper Hook*
540 She throws away his crutches when he is trapped in a fire in their house, although he does survive.

55. CATCHPHRASES
541 John Wayne in *The Searchers* (1956)
542 Paul Newman in *Butch Cassidy and the Sundance Kid* (1969)
543 John Wayne in *Big Jake* (1971)
544 Jack Palance in *Shane* (1953)
545 Tom Selleck in *Monte Walsh* (2003)

546 James Stewart in *Destry Rides Again* (1939)
547 Emilio Estevez in *Young Guns II* (1990)
548 Chief Dan George in *Little Big Man* (1970)
549 Chubby Johnson in *Bend of the River* (1952)
550 John Wayne in *She Wore a Yellow Ribbon* (1949)

56. MORE WESTERN OSCARS
551 Melvyn Douglas (best supporting actor) and Patricia Neal (best actress).
552 Ten, winning none.
553 Four: best screenplay, best song, best cinematography, best music.
554 Dimitri Tiomkin
555 Cinematography (Loyal Griggs).
556 *She Wore a Yellow Ribbon* (1949)
557 Kevin Costner
558 Denzel Washington for best supporting actor.
559 James Wong Howe
560 Best Sound

57. REMAKES
561 Alex Cord
562 *The Paleface* (1948)
563 *The Asphalt Jungle* (1950)
564 *Outland*
565 *Gunga Din* (1939)
566 James Arness
567 Tom Tryon
568 *Seven Samurai* (1954)
569 Paul Newman
570 *Broken Lance*

58. THE 1950S
571 Angie Dickinson and *Rio Bravo*.
572 DeForest Kelley
573 They were all filmed in 3-D.
574 Martin and Lewis (Dean and Jerry)
575 A bullwhip

576 *A Man Alone*
577 John Wesley Hardin
578 Robert Aldrich
579 A Sioux ritual in which the quarry is given a start the length of one arrow shot. The quarry is then chased until he is caught or escapes.
580 Mexico

59. THE GREAT WESTERN DIRECTORS: BUDD BOETTICHER
581 True
582 Floating poker games.
583 Burt Kennedy
584 Elmore Leonard
585 *Two Mules for Sister Sara* (1970)
586 He sets fire to the tree upon which his wife was hanged.
587 Robert Ryan and Rock Hudson
588 Robert Mitchum
589 *Seven Men from Now* (1956)
590 Clint Eastwood

60. WESTERN ICONS: HENRY FONDA
591 1905 in Nebraska
592 *Young Mr Lincoln* and *Drums Along the Mohawk*
593 *The Hired Hand*
594 George Armstrong Custer
595 He shot and killed a young boy.
596 *Big Hand For a Little Lady* (1966)
597 To have a shave.
598 *The Rounders*
599 *Firecreek* (1968) and *The Cheyenne Social Club* (1970)
600 *The Oxbow Incident* (1943)

61. UNSUNG
601 Ricky Nelson
602 Fabian
603 Frankie Avalon

604 Roy Orbison
605 Glen Campbell
606 Bobby Darin
607 Willie Nelson
608 Iggy Pop
609 Jewel
610 Kris Kristofferson

62. GREAT WESTERN BAD GUYS (PHOTO)
611 Sheb Wooley (left) and Robert Wilke
612 Lee Marvin
613 Leo Gordon
614 Jack Palance
615 Stephen McNally
616 Richard Boone
617 Arthur Kennedy
618 Lee Van Cleef
619 Dan Duryea
620 Jack Elam

63. THEY TURNED IT DOWN
621 Butch
622 Cary Grant
623 Lee Marvin
624 Marlon Brando
625 Jeremy Irons
626 Jack Elam
627 Glenn Ford
628 Will Kane in *High Noon*
629 Kid Shelleen in *Cat Ballou*
630 Deke Thornton

64. NAME THE MOVIE (CAST)
631 *Warlock* (1959)
632 *The Way West* (1967)
633 *One Eyed Jacks* (1961)
634 *The Misfits* (1961)
635 *Hombre* (1967)

636 *Wild Rovers* (1971)
637 *The Tall Men* (1955)
638 *Appaloosa* (2008)
639 *Duel at Diablo* (1966)
640 *The Bravados* (1958)

65. THE1960s
641 Burt Lancaster, Lee Marvin, Robert Ryan, Woody Strode
642 Stanley Kubrick
643 *The Misfits* (1961)
644 Cinerama
645 He had a false metal nose.
646 Burt Reynolds
647 William Goldman
648 *Duel at Diablo* (1966)
649 Will Penny in *Will Penny* (1968)
650 Australia

66. "B" WESTERNS
651 Roy Rogers and Dale Evans
652 Stony Brooke
653 He used a bullwhip to great effect.
654 Buster Crabbe
655 Bullet
656 William Boyd
657 Gene Autry
658 Wild Bill Elliott
659 George (Gabby) Hayes. He was Hopalong Cassidy's
    sidekick.
660 John Wayne

67. THE GREAT WESTERN DIRECTORS: JOHN FORD
661 False—he was born in Maine in 1894
662 Francis Ford
663 *The Man who shot Liberty Valance* (1962)
664 None
665 Arson
666 John Martin Feeney

667 Rear Admiral
668 Orson Welles
669 In the river.
670 *Hangman's House* (1928)

68. TAGLINES
671 *The Beautiful Blonde from Bashful Bend* (1949)
672 *Once Upon a Time in the West* (1968)
673 *The Outlaw Josey Wales* (1976)
674 *The Good, the Bad and the Ugly* (1966)
675 *The Searchers* (1956)
676 *The Man Who Shot Liberty Valance* (1962)
677 *High Noon* (1952)
678 *Butch Cassidy and the Sundance Kid* (1969)
679 *The Wild Bunch* (1969)
680 *Brokeback Mountain* (2005)

69. STUDIOS
681 MGM — *The Naked Spur*
682 Miramax — *Dead Man*
683 RKO — *Fort Apache*
684 Republic — *Rio Grande*
685 Warner Brothers — *Unforgiven*
686 Universal — *Destry Rides Again*
687 Columbia — *Comanche Station*
688 United Artists — *The Magnificent Seven*
689 Paramount — *Shane*
690 Twentieth Century Fox — *The OxBow Incident*

70. REAL LIFE
691 Dean Jagger
692 Pamela Reed
693 Walter Brennan
694 Walter Pidgeon
695 Joel McCrea
696 Paul Newman
697 Paul Newman
698 Victor Mature

699 Dennis Quaid
700 Raymond Massey

71. CATTLE BARONS

701 Donald Crisp	*The Man from Laramie*
702 Ed Asner	*El Dorado*
703 Spencer Tracey	*Broken Lance*
704 Jason Robards	*Comes a Horseman*
705 Jeannie Crain	*Man Without a Star*
706 Barbara Stanwyck	*Forty Guns*
707 Walter Huston	*The Furies*
708 Brian Keith	*The Rare Breed*
709 Billy Green Bush	*The Culpepper Cattle Company*
710 Lionel Barrymore	*Duel in the Sun*

72. THE GREAT WESTERN DIRECTORS: SERGIO LEONE

711 *The Good, the Bad and the Ugly*
712 *Ben Hur*
713 *Yojimbo* (1961)
714 Spain
715 Blondie rescues Tuco from the attentions of bounty hunters.
716 He dons a breastplate of armour.
717 Monument Valley
718 In a cemetery
719 Ennio Morricone
720 *Once Upon a Time in the West*

73. FEMME FATALES

721 Joan Crawford
722 Valerie French
723 Veronica Lake
724 Marie Windsor
725 Marlene Dietrich
726 Jennifer Jones
727 Audrey Totter
728 Denise Darcel
729 Dorothy Malone
730 Susan Hayward

74. WESTERN STALWARTS 1

731 Ward Bond

732 Glenn Ford

733 Burt Lancaster

734 James Garner

735 Richard Farnsworth

736 John Ireland

737 Joanne Dru

738 *True Grit* and *Butch Cassidy and the Sundance Kid*

739 Gregory Peck, who grew a moustache for his role of Jimmy Ringo in The Gunfighter. Producer Darryl Zanuck reckoned that a clean shaven Peck would have helped the film take more box office.

740 Robert Ryan

75. WESTERN ICONS: BEN JOHNSON

741 *Wagon Master* (1950)

742 *The Wild Bunch* (1969)

743 *The Undefeated* (1969)

744 *Chisum* (1970)

745 *Shane* (1953)

746 *Bite the Bullet* (1975)

747 *Major Dundee* (1965)

748 *She Wore a Yellow Ribbon* (1949)

749 *One Eyed Jacks* (1961)

750 *Rio Grande* (1950)

76. THE 1970s

751 *Blazing Saddles* (1974)

752 The James-Younger gang

753 *Bite the Bullet* (1975)

754 Tim McIntire, son of John.

755 Alan Sharp

756 Tom Berenger (Butch) and William Katt (Sundance)

757 James Garner

758 *Posse*

759 Keith Carradine with I'm Easy from *Nashville* (1975)

760 *Goin' South*

77. BURT AND KIRK

761 Burt in *Vera Cruz* (1954)
762 Kirk in *The Way West* (1967)
763 Kirk in *Posse* (1975)
764 Burt in *The Hallelujah Trail* (1965)
765 Kirk in *Lonely are the Brave* (1962)
766 Kirk in *The Last Sunset* (1961)
767 Burt in *The Scalphunters* (1968)
768 Burt in *Ulzana's Raid* (1972)
769 Kirk in *Man Without a Star* (1955)
770 Burt in *The Professionals* (1966)

78. THE GREAT WESTERN DIRECTORS: SAM PECKINPAH

771 *The Deadly Companions* (1961)
772 *The Westerner*
773 *My Name is Nobody* (1973)
774 Charlton Heston
775 Don Siegel
776 *The Glory Guys* (1965)
777 *Ride the High Country* (1962)
778 *The Wild Bunch* (1969)
779 Julian Lennon
780 James Coburn. The film was *Affliction*. (1998)

79. WESTERN STALWARTS 2

781   Andrew McLaglen, son of Victor.
782   Robert Taylor
783   Jim Bowie
784   Matt Clark
785   Warren Oates
786   Three (all best supporting actor)
787   Peter Graves
788   Steve Forrest
789   Richard Jaeckel
790   James Coburn

80. MUSICAL WESTERNS
791 *Paint Your Wagon* (1969)
792 *The Harvey Girls* (1946)
793 *Seven Brides for Seven Brothers* (1954)
794 *Oklahoma!* (1955)
795 *Annie Get Your Gun* (1950)
796 *Calamity Jane* (1953)
797 *The Beautiful Blonde from Bashful Bend* (1949)
798 *Red Garters* (1954)
799 *Annie Get Your Gun* (1950)
800 *Paint Your Wagon* (1969)

81. KIDS
801 Brandon De Wilde
802 Claude Jarman Jr.
803 Jenna Boyd
804 Hailee Steinfeld
805 David Ladd
806 Sydney Penny
807 Tommy Rettig
808 Gary Gray
809 Robert Carradine
810 Jon Francis

82. DEATH IN THE WEST
811 He is run over by only the second automobile he has ever seen.
812 "Knocking on Heaven's Door."
813 He puts his harmonica in Frank's mouth.
814 "So long, partner."
815 He froze to death lying in wait for his partner played by Stewart Granger, who he planned to kill.
816 Bruce Dern
817 An axe
818 Dana Andrews, Anthony Quinn, and Francis Ford
819 "I God Woodrow, it's been quite a party, ain't it."
820 He is shot in the back by Hunt (Skip Homier) and Ringo insists that he drew first condemning his murderer to a life much like Ringo has himself led.

83. THE 1980s

821 United Artists

822 Willie Nelson

823 *Stagecoach*. Released in 1986, it starred Willie Nelson, Kris Kristofferson, Johnny Cash, and Waylon Jennings.

824 *Silverado* (Lawrence Kasdan)

825 *Glory*

826 Billy the Kid

827 "Gentleman" Jim Corbett

828 Richard Farnsworth

829 Johnny Cash as Frank and Kris Kristofferson as Jesse.

830 The singing cowboy

84. WESTERN ICONS: CLINT EASTWOOD

831 1930 in San Francisco.

832 Rowdy Yates

833 Hell

834 He is fed poisonous mushrooms by the Southern Belles he has used and manipulated.

835 Don Siegel

836 *High Plains Drifter* (1973)

837 Don Siegel and Sergio Leone.

838 Carmel in Monterey, California.

839 A shoe salesman.

840 *High Plains Drifter*

85. THE GREAT WESTERN DIRECTORS: RAOUL WALSH

841 "Western Noir"

842 A gunsmith

843 *In Old Arizona* (1929)

844 John Wilkes Booth (assassin of Abraham Lincoln)

845 *The Big Trail*

846 *Colorado Territory* (1949)

847 Florida

848 *A Distant Trumpet* (1964)

849 *Pursued* (1947)

850 Sitting Bull (played by Anthony Quinn)

86. GREAT WESTERN CHARACTER ACTORS (PHOTO)
851 Burl Ives
852 Denver Pyle
853 Jay C Flippen
854 Marie Windsor
855 R.G. Armstrong
856 Gibert Roland
857 Katy Jurado
858 Walter Brennan
859 Walter Huston
860 Warren Oates

87. SPAGHETTI WESTERNS 2
861 Burt Kennedy
862 Sergio Corbucci
863 Sergio Leone
864 *Django* (1966)
865 Nathan Van Cleef
866 Burt Reynolds
867 *A Fistful of Dollars* (1964), which was a virtual copy of Kurosawa's Yojimbo.
868 Sergio Leone, who used the name Bob Robertson on release of *A Fistful of Dollars* as he feared American audiences would not want to see an Italian western.
869 *Django* (1966)
870 A machine gun

88. WESTERN ICONS: ROBERT MITCHUM
871 1917
872 Hopalong Cassidy
873 As John Wayne's leading lady
874 *The Good Guys and the Bad Guys*
875 *Tombstone*
876 *Londonderry Air* and *The Cowboy's Lament*
877 *The River of No Return* (1954) Rory Calhoun played Marilyn's husband.
878 Possession of marijuana
879 *El Dorado* (1966)

880 In his bible (Mitchum played a murderous preacher)

89. NATIVE AMERICANS 2
881 The Cheyenne
882 Crow
883 *The Outlaw Josey Wales* (1976)
884 Huron
885 The Sioux Sun Vow Ceremony
886 Iron Eyes Cody
887 Robert Blake. He played the little boy who sold Bogie the winning lottery ticket in 1947's *The Treasure of the Sierra Madre.*
888 The Cheyenne
889 Victor Mature
890 A declaration of war against the U.S. army.

90. THE 1990s
891 They wore a red sash around their waist.
892 He twirls his silver whisky cup in the same manner as Ringo.
893 Neil Young
894 *Cimarron* (1931)
895 Seven
896 Monument Valley
897 Clint Eastwood
898 He performed one-handed press-ups on the Oscar stage.
899 *Havana* (1990)
900 Sam Elliott

91. STRANGE BUT TRUE
901 Wyatt Earp
902 John Kennedy, a detective who foiled a plot to assassinate President Abraham Lincoln.
903 It had no bars.
904 Gregory Peck in *The Gunfighter.*
905 Ward Bond (born 1903) played the father with Joseph Cotton (born 1905) as his son.
906 *A Man Called Horse*
907 A camel

908 She was the voice of the devil in *The Exorcist.*
909 Shenandoah
910 Wyatt Earp

92. THE GREAT WESTERN DIRECTORS: ANTHONY MANN

911 False—he was born Emil Anton Bundesman in 1906 in San Diego. He died in Berlin in 1967.
912 A small bell.
913 Five
914 He has a rope burn on his neck as a result of an attempt to lynch him.
915 They find that Lassoo is a ghost town and the bank is deserted.
916 Stewart's character recues Kennedy who is about to be lynched.
917 Neville Brand in *The Tin Star* (1957)
918 *The Naked Spur* (1953)
919 "You'll be seein' me."
920 A bounty hunter.

93. WESTERN STALWARTS 3

921 Jack Elam
922 Dan Duryea and John Doucette
923 "Big Boy"
924 Ken Curtis
925 A.C. Lyles
926 Russell Simpson in *My Darling Clementine* (1946)
927 Jeff Chandler in *Broken Arrow* (1950), *The Battle at Apache Pass* (1952), and in an uncredited role in *Taza, Son of Cochise* (1954).
928 His father nicknamed him "Dobe" because his red hair resembled the colour of the adobe soil at Harry Carey Senior's ranch.
929 Slim Pickens
930 True

94. FOREIGN DEPARTURES

931 *Utu*   New Zealand
932 *El Topo*   Mexico

933 *Death Rides a Horse* — Italy
934 *The Treasure of Silver Lake* — Germany
935 *Tears of the Black Tiger* — Thailand
936 *Viva Maria!* — France
937 *The Grey Fox* — Canada
938 *The Proposition* — Australia
939 *The Sheriff of Fractured Jaw* — Great Britain
940 *Sholay* — India

95. WESTERN TURKEYS
941 *Shalako* (1968)
942 *The Terror of Texas Town* (1938)
943 *Dirty Dingus Magee* (1970)
944 *Billy the Kid v Dracula* (1966)
945 *Wild Wild West*
946 *Four for Texas* (1963)
947 A set of gold plated false teeth
948 *Charro!*
949 *Wagons East* (1994)
950 *Zachariah* (1971)

96. NAME THAT KID
951 Dustin Hoffman in *Little Big Man* (1970)
952 Audie Murphy in *Night Passage* (1957)
953 Jaimz Woolvett in *Unforgiven* (1992)
954 Gene Wilder in *Blazing Saddles* (1974)
955 Sid James in *Carry on Cowboy* (1965)
956 Scott Brady in *Johnny Guitar* (1954)
957 Audie Murphy in *The Duel at Silver Creek* (1952)
958 Benny Hill, in a sketch from *The Benny Hill Show*.
959 Randolph Scott in *Ride the High Country* (1962) The Oregon Kid is the alias that Scott's character uses in a wild west sideshow.
960 Jackie Chang in *Shanghai Noon* (2000)

97. NAME THE MOVIE
961 *Arrow in the Dust* (1954)
962 *The Hanging Tree* (1959)

963 *Badman's Country* (1958)
964 *They Rode West* (1954)
965 *The Stalking Moon* (1968)
966 *Rio Conchos* (1964)
967 *A Gunfight* (1971)
968 *A Man Alone* (1955)
969 *The Good Guys and the Bad Guys* (1969)
970 *Blood on the Moon* (1948)

98. THE WESTERN AIN'T DEAD YET: TWENTY-FIRST CENTURY WESTERNS

971 Ed Harris
972 James Mangold
973 *Blackthorn*
974 Nick Cave
975 Tommy Lee Jones
976 Wyatt Earp
977 Pierce Brosnan
978 Johnny Depp
979 Frank James and Cole Younger
980 Christoph Waltz

99. THE GREAT WESTERN DIRECTORS: HOWARD HAWKS

981 1896
982 A finger
983 *Rio Lobo* (1970)
984 John Ford
985 *High Noon*
986 *Rio Bravo*
987 Edgar Allan Poe
988 *Red River*
989 Gary Cooper
990 *Red River*

100. GREAT WESTERN CHARACTER ACTORS

991 Ward Bond
992 Strother Martin

993 Royal Dano
994 Edgar Buchanan
995 Slim Pickens
996 Claude Akins
997 John McIntire
998 Frank Ferguson
999 Ray Teal
1000 Paul Fix

101. WESTERN SPEAK

1001 Someone, usually a gambler who pretends to have money, influence or ability.
1002 To ambush someone with intent to kill.
1003 A bluffer particularly relating to poker, or a person who makes empty claims.
1004 Derogatory term applied to northerners who went south after the civil war for political or financial gain.
1005 A young or inexperienced person.
1006 A derogatory term for a farmer.
1007 A small round corn cake, which can be baked or fried.
1008 A hanging or lynching.
1009 An easterner or city person out west.
1010. Bad liquor.

102. CONTEMPARY WESTERNS

1011 Four: best picture, best director, best supporting actor, and best adapted screenplay.
1012 They are to be butchered for dog meat.
1013 To sell the cattle before the government slaughter them.
1014 Larry McMurtry and *Horseman Pass By*
1015 John Sayles
1016 *Thunderheart*
1017 1940s
1018 *Bad Day at Black Rock* (1955)
1019 Breakfast Cereal
1020 Cormac McCarthy

103. WESTERN ICONS: AUDIE MURPHY

1021 1924 in Texas

1022 *The Kid from Texas* (1950)

1023 *Destry*

1024 *Night Passage* (1957)

1025 *No Name on the Bullet* (1959)

1026 *To Hell and Back*

1027 During world war two, he became the most decorated U.S. soldier of all time.

1028 *The Guns of Fort Petticoat* (1957)

1029 *A Time for Dying* (1969)

1030 Audie Murphy died in a plane crash in 1971.

104. NAME THE YEAR

1031   1952

1032   1970

1033   1958

1034   1959

1035   1959

1036   1954

1037   1973

1038   1969

1039   1994

1040   1948

105. WESTERN LOCATIONS

1041 Durango

1042 The Monterey Peninsula in California.

1043 The Animas River Durango, Colorado

1044 *Electra Glide in Blue*

1045 The Grand Tetons

1046 The Rocky Mountains Colorado

1047 Monument Valley

1048 New Mexico

1049 Almeria

1050 The Alabama Hills in California (specifically Lone Pine)

106. A MAN'S (OR A WOMAN'S) GOTTA DO. . .
1051 *Nevada Smith* (1966)
1052 *Rancho Notorious* (1952)
1053 *The Bravados* (1958)
1054 *One Eyed Jacks* (1961)
1055 *Hannie Caulder* (1971)
1056 *Last Train from Gun Hill* (1959)
1057 *Shoot Out* (1971)
1058 *The Shooting* (1966)
1059 *The Revengers* (1972)
1060 *Valdez is Coming* (1971)

107. LUST IN THE DUST!
1061 *Duel in the Sun* (1946)
1062 Gregory Peck and Jennifer Jones
1063 King Vidor
1064 The lovers shot each other to death on top of a mountain.
1065 Divine
1066 "Wing Ding Tonight"
1067 Rio
1068 Two Reasons
1069 'U' certificate
1070 Howard Hughes

108. CLINT'S QUOTES
1071 *High Plains Drifter* (1973)
1072 *A Fistful of Dollars* (1964)
1073 *Unforgiven* (1992)
1074 *The Outlaw Josey Wales* (1976)
1075 *Two Mules for Sister Sara* (1970)
1076 *The Good, the Bad, and the Ugly* (1966)
1077 *Joe Kidd* (1972)
1078 *For a Few Dollars More* (1965)
1079 *Unforgiven* (1992)
1080 *The Outlaw Josey Wales* (1976)

109. WESTERN ICONS: GLENN FORD
1081 In 1916 in Quebec
1082 Eleanor Powell
1083 Shirley MacLaine
1084 *Othello*
1085 *Lust for Gold*
1086 Brazil
1087 *Cade's County*
1088 *3:10 to Yuma* (1957)
1089 Harrison Ford
1090 Rhonda Fleming

110. CLASSIC WESTERN SCENES
1091 John Wayne in *Stagecoach* (1939)
1092 *Ulzana's Raid* (1972)
1093 *The Great Train Robbery* (1903) The actor was George
    Barnes.
1094 *Rio Bravo* (1959)
1095 *The Man from Laramie* (1955)
1096 Charlton Heston and Gregory Peck in *The Big Country*
    (1958)
1097 *Johnny Guitar* (1954)
1098 *Ride the High Country* (1962)
1099 *The Wild Bunch* (1969)
1100 *Bad Day at Black Rock* (1955) and Ernest Borgnine

111. BEHIND THE SCENES
1101 Yakima Canutt
1102 Frank Nugent
1103 *Butch Cassidy and the Sundance Kid*
1104 *Stagecoach*
1105 Tex Ritter
1106 Andre Previn
1107 Lucien Ballard
1108 Walter Wanger
1109 Max Steiner
1110 Chuck Robertson

112. WESTERN ICONS: RICHARD WIDMARK

1111 In 1914 in Sunrise Township Minnesota.

1112 *Backlash* (1956)

1113 Spencer Tracy

1114 *Yellow Sky* (1948), which was Widmark's first western. The character's name was Dude. Dean Martin played Dude in *Rio Bravo*.

1115 "I was gonna hand you yours."—in reference to Robert Taylor throwing Widmark's gun away.

1116 True (Green City, Missouri)

1117 Widmark's character died at the climax of all of them.

1118 Two (*Two Road Together* in 1961 and *Cheyenne Autumn* in 1964)

1119 He is stabbed in his gun hand.

1120 In 2008 aged ninety-three.

113. DUKES QUOTES

1121 *The Searchers*

1122 *True Grit*

1123 *McLintock!*

1124 *Rio Bravo*

1125 *El Dorado*

1126 *Stagecoach*

1127 *The Shootist*

1128 *The War Wagon*

1129 *The Searchers*

1130 *Stagecoach*

114. REVISIONIST WESTERNS

1131 *The Man from Laramie* (1955)

1132 Abraham Polonsky

1133 Jeff Bridges

1134 He is shot and dies in a snowdrift with Leonard Cohen's "Winter Lady" on the soundtrack.

1135 *The Jack Bull*

1136 Shit For Luck

1137 *Open Range*

1138 *The Shooting* and *Ride in the Whirlwind*

1139 *The Wild Bunch*
1140 Wild Bill Hickok

115. EXPERT WESTERN STALWARTS
1141 He played a vampire gunslinger who could only be killed with a bullet containing a sliver of the true cross from the crucifixion.
1142 Julie Adams
1143 Strother Martin
1144 Paul Fix
1145 Jack Lambert
1146 Don "Red" Barry
1147 Jack Palance
1148 George Kennedy
1149 "Rocky," and his horse was called Black Jack.
1150 Dorothy Malone

116. EXPERT CLINT
1151 *For a Few Dollars More*
1152 *A Fistful of Dollars*
1153 Colt Walker 1847
1154 Phil Kaufman
1155 The Bible.
1156 Clint drives a train off its rails and through a saloon.
1157 *The Outlaw Josey Wales*
1158 Arizona
1159 Carrie Snodgrass who appears in the film had a relationship with Neil Young in the 1970s.
1160 John Vernon as Fletcher

117. EXPERT WESTERN QUOTES
1161 *High Noon* (Katy Jurado)
1162 *The Outlaw Josey Wales* (Chief Dan George)
1163 *They Died with Their Boots On* (G.P. Huntley)
1164 *Butch Cassidy and The Sundance Kid* (Ted Cassidy)
1165 *The Magnificent Seven* (Yul Brynner)
1166 *The Gunfighter* (Gregory Peck)
1167 *Johnny Guitar* (John Carradine)

1168 *Once Upon a Time in the West* (Henry Fonda)
1169 *Vera Cruz* (Burt Lancaster)
1170 *Blazing Saddles* (Gene Wilder)

118. EXPERT WESTERN ICONS
1171 John Wayne, James Stewart, and Henry Fonda
1172 Robert Mitchum's son Christopher.
1173 A Palomino
1174 A gun belt and not much else. Wayne calls Douglas "Precious" mimicking Douglas's lady companion.
1175 Clint Eastwood
1176 "I bet that rattler died."
1177 Robert Mitchum
1178 Kirk Douglas in *The Man from Snowy River*
1179 Gary Cooper (1927) and Robert Mitchum (1944) who appeared in different versions of *Nevada*.
1180 Jefferson Cody. He was searching for his wife who had been kidnapped by Comanches.

119. EXPERT JOHN WAYNE
1181 Barbara Streisand
1182 Harry Carey
1183 The Red River "D" belt buckle.
1184 *The Man Who Shot Liberty Valance* (1962)
1185 False. He was born Marion Robert Morrison. His parents changed Robert to Mitchell after Duke's brother was born and he was named Robert.
1186 *The Comancheros* (1961)
1187 Michael Morris. The episode was called "The Colter Craven Story."
1188 James Stewart
1189 *Big Jake* (1971)
1190 "This is my birthday. Give me the best in the house."

120. EXPERT WESTERN TRIVIA
1191 *The Fiend who walked the West* (1958)
1192 James Arness

1193 Althea Gibson was a champion tennis player winning five grand slam titles.
1194 *Once Upon a Time in the West* at over seven minutes.
1195 Three (1914, 1918 and 1931)
1196 James Corbett v Bob Fitzimmons in Carson City in 1897.
1197 Stacey and James Keach as Frank and Jesse James. David, Keith and Robert Carradine as Cole, Jim and Bob Younger. Randy and Dennis Quaid as Clell and Ed Miller. Nicholas and Christopher Guest as Bob and Charlie Ford.
1198 Contention
1199 *Battle Beyond the Stars*
1200 Robert Vaughn

121. EXPERT CLASSIC WESTERNS
1201 *Stagecoach*
1202 James Stewart (twice), Stephen McNally (twice), John McIntire, Rock Hudson, Charles Drake, Dan Duryea. Tony Curtis and Jay C Flippen also briefly handle the gun.
1203 "I'll see you in Hell, William Munny."
1204 Dino notices blood from the man he had shot dripping into a glass of beer from above.
1205 *Little Big Man*
1206 In the original version John Wayne wears his eye patch over his left eye. In the 2011 version, Jeff Bridges has the patch over his right eye.
1207 Carl Foreman
1208 "The Worst! I was aiming at the horse!"
1209 *Once Upon a Time in the West*
1210 James Drury (Billy), John Anderson (Elder), L.Q. Jones (Sylvus), Warren Oates (Henry), and John Davis Chandler (Jimmy).

122. EXPERT TELEVISION WESTERNS
1211 *The Men from Shiloh*
1212 Fess Parker
1213 "Devil" Anse
1214 Robert Urich. He was President Lincoln's bodyguard.
1215 *The Quest*

1216 *Nichols*
1217 Ty Hardin (*Bronco Layne*)
1218 Walter Hill
1219 Stewart Granger
1220 Eric Fleming

123. HOW THE WEST WAS WON
1221 The installation of the transcontinental telegraph system.
1222 Fred MacMurray (Lewis) and Charlton Heston (Clark)
1223 *Into the West*
1224 Spencer Tracy
1225 Jon Hall
1226 Cecil B. DeMille
1227 *The Way West*
1228 Buffalo Bill (Charlton Heston) and "Wild" Bill Hickok (Forrest Tucker)
1229 The building of the first transcontinental railroad in the USA.
1230 The Alamo

124. THE LAST ROUND-UP
1231 *Red Sun*
1232 *Butch Cassidy and the Sundance Kid* (Paul Newman)
1233 Madeleine Stowe, Andie MacDowell, Mary Stuart Masterson, and Drew Barrymore.
1234 *Return of the Seven* (1966), *Guns of the Magnificent Seven* (1969) and *The Magnificent Seven Ride!* (1972)
1235 *Raiders of the Lost Ark*
1236 *Cowboy* (1958)
1237 Zane Grey
1238 The gunfight at the OK Corral.
1239 Leonard Nimoy
1240 Best original screenplay.

125. CLOSING LINES
1241 *The Good, the Bad, and the Ugly* (1966)
1242 *Hombre* (1967)
1243 *Ride the High Country* (1962)

1244 *Duel in the Sun* (1946)
1245 *Red River* (1948)
1246 *Butch Cassidy and the Sundance Kid* (1969)
1247 *True Grit* (1969 version)
1248 *The Outlaw Josey Wales* (1976)
1249 *Unforgiven* (1992)
1250 *Vera Cruz* (1954)

Lightning Source UK Ltd.
Milton Keynes UK
UKHW022050150222
398742UK00006B/592